YOUNG READER'S BOOK OF CHURCH HISTORY

FREDERICK NORWOOD

WITH JO CARR

Illustrated by Tom Armstrong

ABINGDON • NASHVILLE

THE YOUNG READER'S BOOK OF CHURCH HISTORY

Library of Congress Cataloging in Publication Data

NORWOOD, FREDERICK ABBOTT.
    Young reader's book of church history.
        Bibliography: p.
        Summary: Presents a collection of stories for young readers which relates the history of Christianity from the time of Jesus Christ to the present.
        1. Church history—Juvenile literature. [1. Christianity—History] I. Title.
BR151.N67   270   81-20505   AACR2

ISBN 0-687-46827-2

MANUFACTURED IN THE UNITED STATES OF AMERICA

To
Nicholas, Abigail, and Zachary,
who soon will be old enough to read this book

THE CHAPTERS OF THIS BOOK

Preface.. 9
1. Skateboarding in the Park............................... 11
2. Bumping into Francis of Assisi....................... 14
3. The Bridge.. 21
4. How the Church Began..................................26
5. How the Church Took Shape......................... 32
6. Two Famous Christians................................. 41
7. By the Skin of Our Teeth...............................48
8. Recess: Being Children................................. 54
9. Kings and Crusades...................................... 60
10. The Age of Faith..67
11. It's Easy to Slide Downhill............................. 75
12. Luther Goes to a Picnic.................................83
13. Fix-up Time...87
14. More Fixing Up.. 93
15. The Hidden Reformation.............................. 103
16. Reform in Merry England............................. 110
17. The Pilgrims and Their Friends.................... 117
18. Recess: Being a Child
      in Early Modern Times............................. 125
19. John Wesley and the Methodist Revival....... 132
20. Land of the Pilgrims' Pride.......................... 141
21. From Sea to Shining Sea............................. 148
22. Other Lands Have Sunlight, Too..................156
23. Guess Who!... 168
      A List of References....................................... 176

PREFACE

When I was a graduate student in church history, my professor experimented successfully with writing a history of Christianity, *The Church of Our Fathers,* for young people of high school age. I learned then that it is possible to tell the story of the church without convoluted vocabulary, difficult abstractions, or theological complexity.

But, said my friends, younger readers cannot grasp concepts of time, the long span of historical eras. I thought otherwise and began to try out stories and chapters with children in Sunday school classes and in our neighborhood. All young readers are used to "once upon a time" and "a long time ago." What troubles them is the accumulation of measurements in years and centuries. But they can be led along the way step by step, like Christian, in John Bunyan's *Pilgrim's Progress.* In that way they can travel from the time of Jesus to their own time, and they can learn and know about both. The time between is the subject of this book.

I wish to acknowledge the help given by the young people of Trinity Church of the North Shore in Wilmette, Illinois; by those of Glenview United Methodist Church; and by some in our neighborhood. Above all, they gave me confidence to go ahead with the effort to bring them into history.

I also acknowledge the important work on the manuscript by Jo Carr, who succeeded in sharpening, rewording, and focusing, without changing the basic approach, structure, and style of this journey across the bridge of time.

Chapter 1

SKATEBOARDING IN THE PARK

The skateboard whizzed down the walk, and Jeff listened with satisfaction to the takatakataka of the wheels going over the seams of the sidewalk, ever faster on the downhill slope. He was lost in his thoughts—how great it was to be out for the summer and to have three whole months of skateboarding ahead before he started seventh grade in the fall. Jeff could hear the clatter of other wheels behind him and knew that Pam and Kristi were on the downhill now. It was a fun course through the park—fast enough to be exciting, curvy enough to be challenging. He thrust his knees slightly to the left to curve around the old statue and listened with relish to the slowing takatakataka of the wheels as the walk leveled off for the uphill curve.

Takataka-ta—Crash! Thud! came the sound of wheels and girls behind him. Kristi yelped, shrilly. Pam groaned.

Jeff whirled around on the skateboard and jumped off, running back toward the statue, nearly colliding with the man who was running down the other path toward the girls.

"Dr. Jackson!" Jeff was relieved to find a grown-up on the scene—relieved that it was his neighbor the professor—relieved to see Kristi standing there, obviously OK—and relieved to see Pam, grinning—even if her grin was a lopsided one and the eyes above it swimmy with tears.

Pam was sprawled on the ground, cradling her knee between her hands. Jeff saw that it was skinned, all right, but not too badly. She had skinned her knees worse before—and so had he. Dr. Jackson flicked a bit of dirt off Pam's knee with his handkerchief and then helped her onto the park bench. "Nasty fall!" he said. "Maybe you'd better rest a minute."

"Thanks," said Pam. "Dumb old statue! I would have been fine if it hadn't been in my way."

Jeff laughed. The way Pam said it made you think she was really accusing the statue of tripping her. He looked up at the statue with new interest. It was bigger than life, carved in stone—a gentle, happy man in a monk's robe, with a little stone bird sitting on his hand.

"Hmmm," Jeff said out loud. "He doesn't really look like the sort of guy who would stick out his foot and *trip* somebody."

Dr. Jackson laughed. "You're right, Jeff," he said. "Francis would never do a thing like that."

Kristi walked around to the front of the statue to look at the name carved in the stone block. "Street Francis of A-sissy," she read.

"It *does* look like *street,* doesn't it?" Dr. Jackson looked over Kristi's shoulder at the sign. "St. is the abbreviation for street. But it is also short for saint. *Saint* Francis of Ah-see-see. Assisi was the name of his hometown."

"Hi, Jeff. Hi, Dr. Jackson. What's going on?"

Jeff grunted a greeting to his brother, Jason, and to Anna, who was with him. "Well, Pam, here, ran into a saint . . . or at least she ran into the statue of one.

12

And it sounds like Dr. Jackson knows quite a bit about him. I was hoping maybe he'd tell us some more."

"Sure!" said Pam. "After all, since this saint fellow lives in our park, we at least ought to know a little bit about him."

"Yes," agreed Kristi. "What's a saint?"

Jason plopped down on the grass, always willing to hear a story. Anna sat beside Pam on the park bench, and Jeff and Kristi perched on the base of the statue. Then they all looked up at Dr. Jackson as if they were expecting him to begin at once.

"Uh . . . well . . . , " Dr. Jackson hesitated.

Gee, Jeff thought, He's been teaching at the college since before I was born. But with just us, maybe he's shy! Aloud, he said, "We didn't mean to put you on the spot or anything—but all this has kind of made us curious. We *would* like to hear some more about this Saint Francis . . . if you wouldn't mind."

Dr. Jackson smiled, and then he sat down on the grass by Jason. "Well, no—I don't mind talking about St. Francis, if it's really okay with you. Actually, he's one of my favorite people from the past—a really great guy. But Kristi, will you hold onto your question 'What's a saint?' for a little while?"

"Sure," Kristi agreed.

Jeff leaned back against the warm stone of St. Francis' robe and settled down to listen.

Chapter 2

BUMPING INTO FRANCIS OF ASSISI

Dr. Jackson cleared his throat, and began: "Ah . . . Saint Francis! God's troubadour, they called him. One writer described him . . . I remember the words . . . 'a lean and lively little man, thin as a thread and vibrant as a bowstring.' "

"Neat!" said Anna. "That sounds neat—like a poem."

"Well, this fellow was a little like a poem himself . . . or like a song. He was born eight hundred years ago—in the midst of medieval times, when knights rode around on white chargers, and even went off to fight in the Crusades.

"But Francis wasn't a knight. He was the son of a wool merchant. His father was out of town when he was born, so his mother named him Giovanni (which is Italian for John) Bernardone. But when Papa Bernardone came home, he said, 'No! We're naming this boy *Francis* . . . little Frenchman!' Francis was a pretty common name after that, but it may be that Papa Bernardone's little boy was the *first* child ever to be named Francis."

"*Was* he French?" Kristi asked.

"No. His mother may have been part French, but he was Italian. Assisi is a little town in Italy, not far from Rome. The country around it is wild and rough, with steep hills and deep valleys. The people had planted the land with olive orchards and vineyards for grapes. But in those long-ago times, many people thought the mountains and forests were full of hidden creatures, fairies and elves and gnomes and demons, and they *knew* there was an occasional wolf.

"Well, Francis was raised as the spoiled son of a well-to-do merchant. I suppose he grew up like the other young people of his time. He probably played outside most of the time, because their houses were small and crowded. He learned the games, songs, dances, and jokes that children have always known and taught one another. We know from old letters that Francis was not a very strong child, but he was fun to be with. And he had a big allowance, so he was something of a leader. Sometimes he made up games about going on Crusades to Jerusalem. Francis had several brothers and sisters, but he was his father's favorite. As a young man, he was graceful and polite, like a nobleman's son. He loved laughter and sang French love songs. He was popular and ran with the liveliest crowd in town. But he still dreamed of becoming a knight and going on a Crusade." Dr. Jackson paused.

"Go, on!" Jeff said. "We haven't got to the famous part yet."

"Well", Dr. Jackson continued, "in that group, it wasn't long before Francis got into trouble. Too much partying, too much wine drinking, too many pranks—like galloping horses through the town, shouting and laughing. Though Francis helped his dad earn money in the wool business, he was even better at *spending* it. Perhaps some of his trouble was with girls. But nobody knows about that. In any case, Francis had his moody ups and downs as a young man—one day he was happy, the next day sad.

"When he was twenty-four, Francis rode off to fight in a local war. But he ended up as a prisoner instead of a hero. He became ill in prison and had a dream, or a *vision,* which changed his life. When he finally came home, he stopped being a wild young man, and he gave up big parties and fancy clothes. He began poking around in the mountain caves outside town, looking for treasure, he said. But some people thought he was under a demon's spell.

"While hiking alone one day in the wooded hills, he found an old ruined *chapel,* or church, and went in to pray. In the middle of his prayers, he heard a voice say, 'Francis, my house is falling to ruins. Go and repair it!' Well, he felt that must have been God speaking, and he set about the task at once. This was both good and bad. It was *good* for the spoiled son of a rich business man to get out and work with his hands, hauling stone and rebuilding the little old church." The professor paused.

"Yeah," said Jeff, "And what was the bad?"

"Well, he took some of his father's wool cloth and sold it to buy building materials. And he gave the money that was left over to buy food for the poor."

"Whoops," said Pam. "I see what you mean about the good and the bad."

"Right," Dr. Jackson went on. "His father was very angry because Francis *kept* taking things without asking, both to fix up the old chapel and to give away. Father/son relations got so bad that Papa Bernardone took Francis to court. Then one day Francis confronted his father in a public place. With the bishop watching, he threw what money he had left on the ground and then stripped off all his clothes. 'These clothes,' he said, 'are not mine. Now I have only a Father in heaven.' The bishop hurriedly got a coat for the naked young man, and Francis

17

went off without a word, away from his home and out of his family. That was very sad. But Francis thought it was what he had to do."

"What about the singing?" Pam asked.

"Francis became a wanderer. Some of the towns-folk would have said he became a tramp. But slowly his wandering took on a purpose. He decided he would spend his life helping people who were poor or sick or unhappy. He would be the 'little brother' of the poor. He would bring the *good* news of the Christian gospel to those who needed it most. Francis had a natural gaity and good humor that kept breaking through. He *sang* as much as he preached —not French love songs, but hymns of praise to God. Francis invented a new way to be God's man. He wanted to live close to the people who needed him and tell them about God. And he wanted to live a simple life. So he gave away everything he had. He wore only a coarse robe, something like a gunny sack, with a rope for a belt. He took nothing with him, but begged for his food. He believed he was doing exactly what Jesus had told his followers to do and that God would take care of him.

"Now, Francis was a good Roman Catholic, so he went to Rome to get the pope's approval of his new way. Pope Innocent III was a great leader of the church, powerful, wise, and already famous. He did not think too much of Francis' simple ideas, but he saw no harm in them and gave his approval. After awhile, other men joined Francis, and that is how the Franciscan order of preaching friars—the Little Brothers—began. It was *easy* to join! All they had to do was throw away their clothes and everything else they owned and get an old brown robe with a rope belt. They would beg for their food, or work for it. But if they were all like Saint Francis, they'd be so full of joy that every now and then, they'd simply burst out in song!"

Dr. Jackson paused, and at just that moment a bird in a nearby tree *did* burst into song! They all laughed! Jason clapped! And then he asked, "Dr. Jack, why is the statue of Francis holding a bird?"

Dr. Jackson smiled. "I like the nickname, Jason!" he said. "About the bird—Francis both *had* and *taught* a deep respect for all God's creatures. He talked to the birds—which isn't really so odd. I've said 'Good morning, bird!' to a robin or two, myself! He called the animals 'Brother'."

"Like Hiawatha did," said Pam.

"Yes. He spoke of the sun and moon as his brother and sister. And fire and water, too. In fact, he wrote a famous hymn just before he died, called 'Canticle to the Sun,' praising God's creation. We have a hymn today that is almost a translation of it." And Dr. Jackson sang one line: "For the beauty of the earth—for the glory of the skies. . . ."

"Well, Saint Francis," said Pam, "you really *were* a nice guy. I'm sorry I ran into you! But I'm glad that now I know who you are."

"Me, too," said Kristi. "If he liked birds, and the earth, and the sun and moon, then the park is a very right place for him to be!"

"Say, Dr. Jack," said Jason, half-grinning as he used the nickname again, "do you know any more stories like that?"

"Yes—do you?" said Kristi. "We could meet here in the park tomorrow and maybe learn about some other saint!"

"Like Street Francis, huh?" teased Jason.

Jeff watched Dr. Jackson, hoping he would agree

to Kristi's proposal. Dr. Jackson looked his way, and Jeff nodded *his* approval.

"Uh . . . well, if you like, I suppose we could do that."

"We'd like!" said Jeff. "We'd like!"

Chapter 3

THE BRIDGE

Jeff was the last to arrive. Dr. Jackson was talking to Jason about the difference between *history* and *legend;* and that either could be told as a *story.*

"Just so it's a *story,*" said Pam. "*Everybody* likes stories."

Dr. Jackson laughed gently. "That's why I think everybody ought to like history," he said.

Jeff was thinking about history class at school. "Sometimes it depends on the story*teller,*" he said.

"Well, yes—and on the story itself. *Church* history is full of good stories. But I think if you all really want to go into this" . . . he paused, and they nodded, Go ahead, Yes . . . "then we ought to make some sort of diagram to keep the stories in order.

"Yesterday we talked about Francis of Assisi. He was a famous Christian of early times. He was so good and so loving that the church has called him a saint. But he was only one of many Christians who lived between the time of Jesus and our time today. You already know that we can read about Jesus in the Bible, especially in the Gospels—Matthew, Mark, Luke, and John.

"But that was long ago, so many years ago that we have a hard time thinking about how long it was. In Sunday school you can learn about Jesus and about others in the *very* early church. And of course you learn about being Christian *today*. But you don't hear too many stories about the long, long time in between—from Jesus way back then, to us now. How did the Christian story of Jesus get all the way from there to here?" They all shook their heads, agreeing to a general gap in their knowledge of church history.

"Well, here is one way to think about it. Imagine a great big bridge, stretching across a broad sea." Jeff and the others crowded around to watch Dr. Jackson, while he scratched a picture on the sandy ground where no grass grew.

"Now, think of this bridge as the way to get from Jesus' time to our time. Over here on the left is the *old* end of the bridge. There is Jesus, at that end." Dr. Jackson drew a stick figure that made Anna laugh. "I'll put a halo over his head to show he is Jesus. In ancient and medieval art, a halo showed that someone was a saint or a holy person. Now here, way over at the other end of the bridge, is where we are—see, all six of us. No haloes."

"No haloes for Pam and Kristi," laughed Jason, teasing.

"No," retorted Kristi. "Or you, either."

"Or any of us," Dr. Jackson agreed.

Jeff was looking at the sketch in the sand. "That's an arch bridge," he commented.

"Right," said Dr. Jackson. "How did you know that?"

"Oh, I studied arch and beam and suspension bridges while I was working on a Scout badge. This one's unusual though, to have *three* arches."

"Right again, Jeff," Dr. Jackson replied. "I drew three arches to show the three divisions of time between Jesus and us. Each time span has a name. The oldest one, nearest Jesus, we call *ancient* history. That means the story of olden times. The middle one, we call *medieval* history. The last arch, nearest us, is the *modern* era. Each of those arches represents a long time, time enough for many generations of grandparents and parents and children and grandchildren to be born and grow old."

"Where is Francis on that bridge, Dr. Jack?" asked Pam.

"He's right here, about the middle of the big middle arch. About half way from Jesus to us, you see." So there was the bridge, with Jesus at one end, five children and a college professor at the other end, and a lonely figure all by himself in the middle.

"Was that the time of King Arthur and Merlin the magician?" asked Anna.

"Not *too* far away. The King Arthur legends took place during the sixth century, a few hundred years before Francis."

We've got a story about olden times at home," said Kristi. "It's about a boy named Cedric, Cedric the Forester. Where does he come?"

"Well, I don't know whether Cedric was a real boy or a fictional boy, but he might have lived around Francis' time. He would not have lived in Italy, though, judging by his name, but in England. It was during the time of knights and armor and swords."

"There were a lot of people going over that bridge, weren't there, Dr. Jack?" commented Pam thoughtfully.

"We can talk about all those people these summer afternoons. Let's meet at *my* house tomorrow—right across the street from Jeff and Jason. I'll make a better sketch of the bridge. You can help draw all the people as we go along."

"You and Anna better do the drawing," said Jeff. "Some of the rest of us aren't too good at it."

"Maybe we are each expert in different areas," said Dr. Jack. "You're the one who knows something about bridges!"

Chapter 4

HOW THE CHURCH BEGAN

Jeff knocked on Dr. Jackson's door and waited on the porch with the others. The summer sun was hot. The cool of the shade and the bit of breeze on the porch felt good.

The door opened, and Dr. Jackson came out to greet his young visitors. "Good!" he said. "I was hoping you could all come today. How about staying out here on the porch?"

"Sure!" "Great." They all scrambled for porch swing and bannister, and Dr. Jackson settled down in the rocker.

"Where were we?" he asked.

"Bridges!" said Jason.

"Jesus," said Anna.

"Early Christians," said Pam.

"History!" said Kristi.

Jeff laughed. "Everybody has a different answer!"

Dr. Jackson laughed, too. "Everybody's right," he said. "We will start with those years close to Jesus' time, right at the beginning of our time bridge." He picked up a roll of butcher paper leaning against the door frame. "I drew it for us. See? The church goes and grows across the long bridge. Stories were passed along about what Jesus had done and what he had taught. Leaders like Paul wrote to the little groups of Christians in Palestine and the other places, and especially in Greece. Paul said that faith in Jesus was not only for Jews, but for everybody."

"But what about the Romans?" asked Jeff. "They were the real rulers all over, weren't they?"

"Yes, but the Romans were pretty mixed up for a while about these new Christians. Remember Pilate, who was the Roman official in Jerusalem? He didn't know what to do with Jesus, and he finally let the crowd decide. Most of all, the Romans wanted to avoid trouble and keep law and order. At first they thought that Christians were just a new sort of Jew. But years went by, and the Christians became more and more different. One Roman governor, Pliny, wrote to the emperor to ask his advice. He didn't know what to do with these strange people. They weren't really criminals. But their teaching just didn't sound right.

"Governor Pliny couldn't decide if it was against the law just to *be* a Christian. Should he punish them just because they were Christian, or only if they did something wrong? They were so . . . well . . . *so different*. They would not worship Roman gods, because, like the Jews, they said there was only one God. And then, too, some of their sayings really were disturbing. For example, Peter said that they must obey God rather than men. A good Roman citizen ought to obey the emperor! And one of the Christian letters said that Christians 'desire a better country, that is, a heavenly' one (Heb. 11:16). That sounds as if they were *against* Rome. Are they planning a revolution? Besides, said Pliny, they are stubborn. Christian sculptors can carve fine animals, but they won't carve images of the gods. Lots of them refuse to be soldiers in the army, because they don't believe in fighting. They aren't *like* other people! Christians are just *too different*."

Dr. Jackson stopped a minute to explain. "Sometimes people are *afraid* of things that are new and different. So they decided to stop Christianity—to wipe it out!

"Roman rulers began to *persecute* the Christians to make them give up their different ways or frighten them away; and if that didn't work, they put them in jail or killed them. The Christians decided to keep quiet so they would not be noticed. Jesus had taught his followers not to *try* to get into trouble. Trouble would come soon enough.

"There were some early Christians in the city of Rome, the capital city of the Roman Empire. Almost two hundred years had now gone by since the time of Christ, and the persecutions were getting worse. To stay away from the Roman police, they hid in caves called *catacombs*, dug in the soft *tufa* rock under the streets. The Christians had dug the caves themselves, in earlier years, for burial places for those who died. There were secret entrances, so now they used the caves as meeting places—safe places where they could hide, where they could worship, where they could keep their most precious things. Some of the people painted pictures on the walls. They were pictures they did not dare make outside, because they were about the Christian faith. This was really the earliest Christian art. The pictures were not fancy. They were only scratched on the cave walls. If you visit these ancient catacombs, you can still see some of them. One is the very first picture of Jesus and his mother. There is a star, and Mary has a veil and plain clothes. There is also a picture of the wise men bringing gifts to the baby Jesus. But there are only *two* wise men, not three."

Dr. Jackson stopped talking for a minute, and it was quiet there on the porch. He took his pen out of his pocket . . . and on the bottom of the paper where he had drawn the bridge, he drew a curved line. Then he handed the pen to Jeff, and their eyes met for long minute. Jeff knew the password. He had seen "the sign of the fish" before, in a church school class. He took the pen and drew another curved line on the paper to complete the fish. And a little shiver went up his back.

Dr. Jackson began to talk again, in a slow and thoughtful way. "We live in a time when we don't have to be afraid of very much. Can you imagine what it would be like to be so afraid that you had to hide to have a church service? Or to have a funeral? Or to baptize a baby? Or to take Communion? Hide in caves, in the dark . . . with somebody standing guard at every entrance to warn you if the soldiers came? Did you know that's why we have *ushers* in churches today? That is a tradition handed down to us from the church of the catacombs. And there is another tradition. Jason, aren't you an acolyte at your church?"

"Sure," said Jason. "We take turns, but I light the candles once a month or so."

"Well, in the catacomb, the acolyte was *very important*. The underground passageways were dimly lit by shafts dug in the *tufa* for ventilation. But there wasn't enough light to see very well. The acolyte's candles were really needed so that the leader could read aloud from one of the letters of Paul or Peter, or from a Scripture. And they were needed so that the others could see the speakers. Acolytes and ushers had extremely important and dangerous jobs."

29

Jason's eyes were bright as he listened—and again Jeff felt a shiver go up his back.

"Did all the Christians get hurt?" Kristi wanted to know.

"No, most of them did not. Trouble might break out at one place, but not at other places. Sometimes years would go by without any persecution. But if the Roman soldiers caught them when they were worshiping and demanded that they worship Roman gods, or the emperor himself, instead—they had trouble.

"All this persecution lasted a long time—about three hundred years, actually." Dr. Jackson stopped again. "Hmm," he said, "Do you have any idea how long that is?"

Jeff thought. It seemed like a fairly long time, all right.

Anna said, "How 'bout when my great, great grandmother was a little girl?"

"That's a good way to measure time, Anna—in generations. But you'd have to add at least eight more 'greats.' Three hundred years ago is about when your great, great, great, great, great, great, great, great, great, great grandmother was a girl."

"Wow," said Jason. "You'd think the Christians would have given up, after being persecuted all those years!"

"If they had," Dr. Jackson reminded them, "the bridge would have been broken, and there would be no church today. But they kept the faith, and they passed it down to us."

Jeff was still thinking about three hundred years. "Why, the United States is only a little over *two* hundred years old." Three hundred years of hiding, and dying, and staying faithful!

"How did the persecutions ever end, Dr. Jack?" Anna asked.

"Well, I guess there were *two* reasons. For one thing, the Romans saw they weren't going to get rid of the Christians that way. They were a problem that would divide the Empire, if the Romans didn't include them in it. And too, more and more people were becoming Christian. Finally, a new emperor, Constantine, decided that Christianity was not a bad thing. He made a new law that Christians could live freely all over the Roman Empire, along with all the other citizens. This happened in the year A.D. 313. That is a date to remember—A.D. 313—when Roman persecution of Christians ended. Then Christian churches grew so much that after awhile Christianity became the official religion of the whole Empire. Now everybody was *supposed* to be Christian. I'm sorry to say that then Christian officials put non-Christians in jail. The persecuted had become the persecutors. That happens sometimes in history."

"Gee," said Anna. "You'd think they'd remember what it felt like."

"Some did," Dr. Jackson said. "But another generation had gone by . . . and by then, who remembers?" He began to roll up the paper. And then he said, "You know, part of the story today was sad, a bad part of history. Should I tell you only the good parts, or should I tell you the bad parts, too?"

"Oh, tell us both good and bad, Dr. Jack," replied Jeff quickly. "Most true stories I know *have* both good and bad parts. That's the way it is."

31

Chapter 5

HOW THE CHURCH TOOK SHAPE

Jeff pulled out a tender grass stem and twirled it between his palms. It was pleasant in the park, and the grass felt cool in the shade near Francis' statue. He watched the girls turning cartwheels with varying degrees of grace and stretched out to enjoy his own laziness. Sun, and summer, and the prospect of Dr. Jack's stories about the past were enough to make him content.

Jason and Dr. Jackson came into the clearing together, finishing up some kind of conversation about cardinals—or rather about *the* Cardinals, Jeff decided, as he heard Jason say something about batting averages.

Dr. Jackson said "Hi" to everyone as they gathered around, then cleared his throat and started right in on the topic for the day.

"Today I'd like for us to talk about how the church began to grow," Dr. Jackson was saying. "The apostles were the first leaders, but what happened when they were gone? Remember, the apostles had lived with Jesus, and that gave them authority. But they grew old, and most of them were killed. Now who would be the leaders? And how would people sort out true Christian teaching from false teaching? People began to teach *different* things. Who would decide what's right? Who would decide how Christians should worship ... and what they should *believe?*"

"How did the apostles die, Dr. Jack?" asked Jason.

"Well, we don't really know for sure. There are old stories about all of them, but we don't know how many are true. We think that both Peter and Paul went to Rome to help start the church there, and probably they both were killed during the first wave of persecutions, under Nero. The legend is that Peter was crucified upside down because he said he was not worthy to die the same way Jesus had. Thomas may have been killed in southern India. They were all gone and leaders were needed, so other men became leaders, or *ministers,* in the churches. In Egypt these ministers, or *elders,* chose one from among themselves to be their *bishop,* or the 'head minister' for a group of churches. One early Christian writer, Irenaeus, said that the bishops were the direct successors of the apostles, each chosen by an apostle to lead after he himself was gone. At Rome, the bishop was especially important, because he was the successor of Peter, who was so often the spokesman for the apostles. Jesus once called Peter the rock on which the church was to be founded. Later on, the Roman Catholic Church said that because of this the bishop of Rome was the leader of all the bishops. But this idea took a long time to grow. Not all the bishops agreed that the Roman bishop was the most important."

"But," broke in Pam, "I thought Jesus said Christians ought to be humble."

"Yes," said Kristi, "but being humble doesn't mean you can't be a leader." The others batted that idea around a bit and finally agreed that there could be such a thing as a humble leader.

"That's a tricky idea, you know," Dr. Jackson commented. "Lots of grown-ups still have problems with it. Anyway, that's how the church began to organize, with leaders and followers, ministers and people. The ministers usually were called *priests*, and some priests became bishops. Finally, most of the Christians in the western part of the Roman Empire agreed that the bishop of Rome was their chief bishop, or *pope*. That wasn't true in the East, though. There, the bishops of Antioch, Alexandria, Jerusalem, and Constantinople were the power figures—all four of them. They were called the *patriarchs*, and the Greek Orthodox Church considered them equal in importance to the pope. It's not that the *four men* in the East and the *one man* in the West were such outstanding *persons*, but rather that those were the important *jobs*. For instance, a king is a powerful figure, even though a *particular* king may be a weak or stupid sort of man.

"Well—enough of organization." Dr. Jackson stood up and walked around, still talking. "Here's another side of the story. What do you do when you are playing a game and disagree about the rules?"

"We argue about it and sometimes get mad," said Jason.

"It's better to find the right rule," said Kristi.

"You have to follow the rules or the game isn't any fun," said Anna.

"Well, Christians found that they weren't clear on the rules. Some said that Jesus was God and only *looked* like a man. Others said Jesus was really only a man whom God chose to be his Son. Others said that he was a great teacher who was *like* God. Christians got into all sorts of arguments about God and Jesus and human beings. How could Jesus be both God and man, both divine and human? The arguments became very complicated, tangled up. Some Christians became angry. It was really hard for them to love one another when they all had different ideas about the faith. Before long, Christians didn't need the Romans to do the persecuting. They were getting pretty good at persecuting one another for having wrong ideas.

"Well . . . how do you settle arguments like that? One way was to come to some agreement on the *true* Christian writings. The Jews had done that when they had decided which writings would be included in the Old Testament, which is basically the Jewish Bible. The Christians had the Old Testament, but they also had the Gospels, telling about the life and teaching of Jesus, plus the letters of Paul and some other writings. These they put together in a *New* Testament, which would be the Christian part of the Bible. 'These books' they said, 'have been given to us by God for our guidance. People wrote the books, but God inspired the writers.' They thought that the writers of the books were either apostles or friends of the apostles. That collection of books, then, became the New Testament, or *canon*. Canon is a Greek word meaning *measuring stick*. This *New* Testament would be the measuring stick by which people could measure ideas, to see which ones were true.

"Another way to test beliefs was to compose a clear statement about what all people should believe. This statement should agree with the Bible and with the teachings of the apostles. We call such a statement a *creed*. The one called the *Apostles' Creed* is the oldest and most famous. The apostles did not write it . . . it wasn't really *written* until the third century. But all its teachings can be found in the New Testament. Most of you probably know it."

I believe in God the Father Almighty, maker of heaven and earth;

And in Jesus Christ his only Son our Lord: who was conceived by the Holy Spirit, born of the Virgin Mary, suffered under Pontius Pilate, was crucified, dead, and buried; the third day he rose from the dead; he ascended into heaven, and sitteth at the right hand of God the Father Almighty; from thence he shall come to judge the quick and the dead.

I believe in the Holy Spirit, the holy catholic Church, the communion of saints, the forgiveness of sins, the resurrection of the body, and the life everlasting. Amen.

"A third way to decide about an idea is to compare it with the experience and wisdom of Christians in the church. If some new teaching disagrees with the things the church taught before, it is probably wrong."

"Hey, wait!" Jeff interrupted. "Not everything new is *wrong*. How can you ever get *good* new thinking into the church?"

"Good question, Jeff. The idea was not to stop new things, but to find the truth. New things that come along with new times and new people are *often* good. Why, just growing up is finding out and getting used to all kinds of new things. But the teachings of Jesus and the things he did can help us *evaluate* the new."

"Yes," said Anna, "I can see that. Some new ideas are crummy—even if everybody's doing it."

"Exactly, Anna," said Dr. Jackson. "And in those early days, when different ideas were being taught, the church decided that teachings and beliefs ought to be measured by the Bible, by the creed, and by the tradition. That is—does the church, at all times, and in all places, teach this?"

Dr. Jackson paused, poked at a weed with his foot, and said, "Let me give you an example of early teachings that Christians finally decided were not good. At that time there was a group called the *Gnostics*. That's a Greek word, too. It's spelled with a G, but pronounced without it. The word means *knowledge,* and the Gnostics thought they had found a secret knowledge. Well, you know it's exciting to share secrets that nobody else knows. And most of you have secrets you won't share with anyone, even your mothers and fathers. We play games with secrets, with codes, with 'pig Latin' and passwords. And it's fun, if it doesn't hurt anyone. But the Gnostics believed they had special secret knowledge about Christ. A lot of people liked the idea, liked being in on the secret. But finally the church said 'No! That is a *heresy*—a false teaching.' Jesus came to tell the good news to all people, not to hide it. What he taught is in the Bible for all to see. He never taught in secret codes or intended to keep anyone out."

That's for sure, Jeff thought. Having secrets just isn't God's way.

"Here's another example," Dr. Jackson went on. "A man named Marcion thought he would revise and purify the Bible, but he had some strange ideas. Marcion believed that there were two Gods. He also believed that the world was bad, and since the Old Testament tells that God created the world, then the Old Testament must be bad, and the God it tells about must be bad, too. So Marcion wanted to throw out the Old Testament and the old God and worship the *new* God. But Marcion didn't like much of the *New* Testament, either. Matthew, Mark, and John didn't suit him. And he liked Luke only if he left out the story of Jesus' birth and all the other parts that

37

mention his family. Paul's letters, and part of Luke should be the Bible—nothing else.

"The Christian leaders got together and decided that Marcion was wrong. They accepted the Old Testament because that had been Jesus' Bible. And they accepted the New Testament because those writings were by the apostles or by their friends. The leaders also agreed on a creed. About three hundred years after Jesus, the church held a great council at Nicaea. From that council came the famous *Nicene Creed*. With changes made later on, it is still used in most Christian churches. It was first directed against another group of *heretics*, or *wrong believers*, the Arians. It said clearly that Jesus Christ was the true Son of God, the same as God."

I believe in one God: the Father Almighty, maker of heaven and earth, and of all things visible and invisible;

And in one Lord Jesus Christ, the only begotten Son of God: begotten of the Father before all worlds, God of God, Light of Light, very God of very God, begotten, not made, being of one substance with the Father, through whom all things were made; who for us men and for our salvation came down from heaven, and was incarnate by the Holy Ghost of the Virgin Mary, and was made man, and was crucified also for us under Pontius Pilate; he suffered and was buried, and the third day he rose again according to the Scriptures, and ascended into heaven, and sitteth on the right hand of the Father; and he shall come again with glory, to judge both the quick and the dead; whose kingdom shall have no end.

And I believe in the Holy Ghost, the Lord, the giver of life, who proceedeth from the Father and the Son, who with the Father and the Son together is

THE CHURCH TOOK SHAPE

worshiped and glorified, who spake by the prophets.
And I believe in one holy catholic and apostolic
Church. I acknowledge one baptism for the remis-
sion of sins. And I look for the resurrection of the
dead, and the life of the world to come. Amen.

"When the church leaders were doing all this, they
were creating *tradition*. These three guideposts—the
Bible, creed, and tradition—would help Christians
know the truth.

"In these ways, slowly the church was formed. The
pope, bishop of Rome, became head of the Roman
Catholic Church in western Europe, and the four
patriarchs were leaders of the Eastern (or
Greek) Orthodox Church in the Middle East. These
churches taught from the Bible, the creed, and the
tradition. If you did not agree with the teachings, you
were called a heretic, even though you were sure
your teaching was true—even if it was in the Bible
and in the teachings of Jesus. To be accepted, it had
to meet all three standards. The church punished
heretics, sometimes by not allowing them to go to
church anymore, sometimes by putting them in
prison, and sometimes by killing them. It was sad
indeed to see Christians killing Christians because
they had different ideas."

"But couldn't they just love and help one another
anyway?" Pam wanted to know. "What if they did
have different ideas?"

"Most Christians today would agree, Pam. But long
ago, people were more positive—sure that they were
right and others were wrong. *Exact* beliefs were very
important to them, important enough to give their
lives for, or to take the lives of others. The important
thing was to worship in the right way and to keep the
faith."

Dr. Jackson sighed. "The Church has had some hard times," he went on. "It has done some harmful things. Maybe the church is like most of *us*—a mixture of some good qualities and some not-so-good ones."

"Yeah," said Jason, "and we're the ones who said tell us the *whole* story, and don't leave out the bad stuff."

Jeff grunted. "Even when it's the good guys that are the bad guys."

Chapter 6

TWO FAMOUS CHRISTIANS

Jason and Jeff were to spread the word: "Tuesday afternoon at Dr. Jack's . . . not at the park this time."

They gathered on the porch again and talked about bees and baseball until Kristi and Pam arrived.

It was Anna who asked the opening question: "Dr. Jack, what happened to our big bridge—the one that goes from Jesus to us?"

"Well," Dr. Jack began, "I have a surprise for you. Come on in."

They all trooped into the house and followed him to the study. There they saw the long sheet of paper on the floor with sketches on it.

"Oh," cried Anna. "Look, there are people on the bridge!"

"This must be Francis," said Eric, pointing to a figure in a friar's robe in the middle.

"And here is Jesus, over here at the beginning," said Pam. "But who is that?" she asked, pointing to an imposing person part way over. "He looks like a king."

"Near enough. That's Emperor Constantine. He was the Roman ruler who stopped the persecution of the Christians. To help you think about time, look at the things on the bridge so far. After the drawing of Jesus, you can see a letter. That's Pliny's letter to the emperor, asking him what on earth to do about these Christians. It was written about a hundred years after the birth of Jesus. And a couple of hundred years after that, came Constantine. He said, 'Leave the Christians alone'—and he even became a Christian himself. It was about that time that the Nicene Creed was written. That is what the scroll, there, is for."

The young people crowded up to the first arch of the bridge, near the figure of Jesus. They looked at the sketches of the people, the letter, and the scroll. Except for Saint Francis and two more new figures, the rest of the bridge was empty.

Pam pointed, "Who are *those* two people?" she asked. "They are over a little, so they must be another hundred years on. One of them sure has a funny hat."

"That's a bishop's hat, I bet," said Anna. "Pope John Paul wears one."

"Those are the two people I want to tell you about today," Dr. Jack said. "Let's just sit here on the library rug."

"The two new men on the bridge are Jerome and Augustine, both very famous. Jerome translated the Bible into Latin, which was the main language in ancient times. The Roman Catholic Church used his translation right down to our own time. And the other man, Augustine, became the most important thinker and writer in the whole history of the Christian church." Dr. Jack stopped a minute, and laughed. "In a way," he said, "Jerome was the *bad* good guy, and Augustine was the *good* good guy."

Jeff chuckled to himself. It sounded as though it would be a neat story.

"Jerome was a *monk*. We will have to talk about *that* first. Some Christians thought that serious followers of Jesus ought to get farther away from the

evil things of life. They thought the world was so bad that they couldn't be good Christians *in* it, so they went *out* of it, to live in the desert. They were called *hermits*. At first, each lived by himself in a cave or hut, to keep away from temptations. But many of them found that their temptations came right along into the desert with them. One of them, Anthony, said he still dreamed about dancing girls. Of course not everyone became a hermit. Many Christians realized that the world was not such a bad place. After all, God made the world for us to live in, and he created people with bodies, and with all kinds of feelings. But the hermits thought the body was bad; so they thought sex was bad. To get rid of such thoughts, they tried all sorts of things, like beating themselves with switches or standing for a long time on one leg. One of them lived for many years on top of a high pillar, pulling up his food with a rope. But that is not a very practical nor a very helpful way to live. Some of the ideas of the old desert hermits were pretty strange. And yet they were very devout people. And some of them have a lot to teach us about *silence*."

"Well," broke in Jason, "they sure thought some things were bad that aren't bad at all!"

"Yes, and after awhile the everyone-alone-on-his-own idea got pretty boring, and hermits began to live together, where they could help one another. They lived in *monasteries,* as monks. A monastery was (and is) a group-living religious house, but only for men. *Convents* were (and are) group-living religious houses for women. Jerome, here, was a monk. Though he was born in the West, he lived most of his life in a monastery in Bethlehem. He felt that his calling was to translate the Bible—that people should have it in Latin, their own language. And he spent incredible hours studying and translating from the old Hebrew."

"Then how come you said he was a *bad* good guy?" Kristi wanted to know.

Dr. Jackson chuckled. "Well, he was a good scholar, but he was a real grouch. He was vain and pig-headed. He called people names and tried to ruin their reputations if they disagreed with him."

"Whew," said Jason. "My Dad would say Jerome was not the sort of guy you'd like to go fishing with."

"Exactly," Dr. Jackson agreed. "He was as disagreeable a saint as ever lived."

"Then how could he be a saint?" Kristi asked.

"Ah! We are back to the question you asked the first day, Kristi. . . . What's a saint? I'm still not ready for us to answer it. But please, when we do try to answer that question, remember old Jerome—a restless, nervous, crotchety, *driven* man, but one who still did an amazing piece of work for the church."

"Is Augustine the *good* good guy?" Pam asked.

"Yes," Dr. Jackson said. "But even *good* guys do some things they aren't too proud of. In one of Augustine's books he tells about the time he and some other boys stole some pears from an orchard. But the pears were not ripe, so the boys threw them all away. It was bad enough to steal, but to throw them away was a terrible waste. At the time, Augustine and the others had considered it a 'fun' thing to do. But he felt bad about it afterward. Sometimes girls and boys taunt each other with 'I dare you,' and do things they wish later they could undo." Dr. Jackson was quiet for a minute and gave them time to follow their own thoughts.

Then he went on. "When Augustine was a young man, he decided to live with the young woman he loved. He didn't *marry* her, because he thought it might keep him from becoming rich and famous. But he lived with her and was faithful to her for fifteen years.

They had one child, a little boy. They named him Adeodatus (A-deo-datus), which in Latin means 'from God given.' After those fifteen years, Adeodatus' mother became a nun, and Augustine himself was deeply troubled about what he wanted to do with his life.

"One day he was sitting in a garden, thinking and worrying, when suddenly he heard a little child, who was playing nearby, chanting in a sing-song voice, 'Tolle, lege, tolle, lege'—'Take up and read, take up and read.' At that moment he saw a copy of the New Testament lying nearby. He picked it up and opened it, and on that page he saw what Paul had written to the Romans: 'No revelling or drunkenness. . . .Let Christ Jesus himself be the armour that you wear' (Rom. 13:13 NEB). The words got through to Augustine. He became a Christian. His mother had prayed all his life that this might happen. And he and Adeodatus were baptized together.

"In time, Augustine became a bishop. He wrote many fine and very helpful books. Some of them were so good that Christians still read them now, fourteen hundred years later. Both Roman Catholics and Protestants think highly of Augustine.

"Like Jerome, Augustine wanted to be a monk. He wanted peace and quiet so that he could study and write. But instead, he was made a bishop. That meant that he was very busy, and in the midst of the world, not separated from it. He didn't think the world was all bad but saw it as a mixture of good and bad. The church itself, he said, is not all good. Nor are all Christians saints. Like the rest of the world, the church and the people in it are a mixture.

"Those were the times when the great Roman Empire was falling apart. Augustine could see that. And he asked one of the biggest questions of all time: Why does God, who made the world, let things fall to pieces? He said the world always had been a place where both good and evil exist, and he used as an example that early Bible story in which Cain, the tough hunter, killed gentle Abel, his brother. Even the Roman Empire, which *had* much good and *did* much good, couldn't last, because there was so much evil in it. But the church will last, in spite of the wickedness that may appear in it from time to time, because God loves the church and has plans for it."

Dr. Jackson stopped and leaned back against his desk with a "that's the end of the story" look.

"That was a good story," said Jason. "I liked hearing something about when Augustine was a boy."

"Yes," said Pam. "Famous people were not famous when they were young. Nobody writes about them until later, so we only get to hear the grown-up parts of their lives."

"Sad, but true," said the professor. "Although I don't think I would want to know from the beginning just how we were all going to turn out."

They joked about that idea. Dr. Jackson pointed to the long stretch of the bridge, with its three big arches. "Next time," he said, "we are going to make a big jump. You see Augustine and Jerome there. Where will we be when we go on from them? What part of the bridge?"

"Middle Ages!" said Pam. "On with the Middle Ages!"

Chapter 7

BY THE SKIN OF OUR TEETH

Dr. Jackson was holding two little lead soldiers in his hand. "I'm going to put them here," he said, "right at the point on our bridge of history where the arch of the ancients meets the arch of the Middle Ages. This is a big turning point in the story of the church—a big change in the lives of people."

"Like starting junior high?" asked Jason, who was especially eager to join his brother, Jeff.

"Well, that's a big change, going from sixth grade in a small school, to a much bigger school halfway across town. Yes, it's a bit like that in our story. We've come to the first big change."

"Wait a minute, Dr. Jack," broke in Jeff. "Isn't this the *second* big change? Didn't the first one come when Constantine said it was OK to be a Christian and stopped the persecutions?"

"Good point, Jeff. And maybe you are right. There are different ways to divide a story. That was a big change all right. But so was the fall of Rome, the collapse of the Roman Empire. That was when the Middle Ages began—when the Roman Empire fell apart and the barbarian tribes came in.

"Some people called those times the Dark Ages, because it seemed that everything was confused, and for the next several hundred years, people would have trouble just staying alive. The times were dangerous. The 'glory that was Greece' and 'the grandeur that was Rome' almost disappeared. Many of the fine books and great works of art were destroyed or lost. That whole way of life was destroyed. Some sculptures and other relics from the old life of Greece and Rome were saved, and you can see them in museums today."

Anna wanted to know, "Who did all that damage, and why?"

"There are at least two answers to that. First, The Roman Empire was getting old and weak. The government became corrupt, and the army, those fine Roman legions, began to lose battles. Things fell apart.

"Second, there were barbarian tribes who migrated west, hunting food and land and wealth. The time came when the Roman army simply couldn't keep them out. They took lands, and captured cities, and broke the Empire apart. Instead of one great empire, for several hundred years there were only smaller kingdoms set up by barbarian chiefs. Out of that came what we call the *feudal system,* with *overlords* who owned the lands, and *serfs* who worked on it."

Pam and Kristi had begun to wiggle, Jeff noticed. Dr. Jackson must have noticed, too, for he plunged at once into a story.

"At the time of the fall of Rome, there was a leader of the church who saved the city from the barbarians. His name was Gregory. He was the pope, the bishop of Rome, the leader of the church for the whole western world. The government had collapsed—there was no king, no army—no one to face the barbarians except Gregory. He would have to do it himself."

"Pretty big job for one guy, huh?" said Jason.

"Indeed it was. The city was out of food. Grain

from Africa was needed. The barbarian Lombards had an army on the way, intending to capture the city. They had already taken many prisoners. Pope Gregory confronted the Lombard leaders and made a deal. If they would leave Rome alone and free the prisoners, he would pay them money. Then he sent ships to Africa for grain and food. The *emperor* was supposed to attend to things like that—not the Pope.

"Pope Gregory was a fine leader for other reasons, too. He did so many things for the church that history has called him Gregory the Great. He sent missionaries to pagan people in different parts of Europe. He encouraged the monks. He improved the form of worship, some of it still used in the Roman Catholic Church. He began to use music for worship, especially that plain form we call the Gregorian chant."

"Where did Gregory's missionaries go?" asked Anna. She loved faraway places, and even the word *missionary* made her back tingle.

"Well, several places," Dr. Jackson said. "Even before Gregory, Christians had taken their faith to other parts of Europe. The first one we hear much about was Patrick, in Ireland."

"Oh, I know about Patrick . . . or sort of," broke in Kristi. "A boy in school is named Patrick—and he says he was named after Saint Patrick who lived a long time ago in Ireland."

"That's the one, Kristi. The Irish call him their patron saint, and they are very proud of him. Actually, he was originally *English,* rather than Irish. He was the son of the mayor in a town in England. When he was sixteen, a horde of Irishmen swooped down on his father's estate, captured him and others, and took them off to Ireland, which was still uncivilized at that time. Patrick spent six years as a slave, herding sheep and pigs. Finally he managed to escape and walked miles and miles to a harbor town where no one would know he was a runaway. There he talked the crew of a trading ship into taking him on board. But it was a wild trip! The boat was driven ashore in a desolate part of England. Patrick and the sailors spent some cold and hungry days making their way back to a town. But there they were captured, and Patrick again was taken prisoner."

"Whew," said Jeff.

Dr. Jackson went on. "Patrick managed to escape again, and he finally reached home. And then—and this is the part that's hard to believe—then he became a priest and *went back to the Irish who had made him a slave*. And he spent the rest of his life bringing the Christian faith to Ireland."

"Hey," said Anna, "that's a lot better story than the snakes-and-shamrocks stuff we *usually* hear about Saint Patrick."

"Right," said Jeff. "I thought the story about driving the snakes out of Ireland was a fake, so I had just sort of crossed Patrick off as being mostly make-believe."

"Well, strange stories *do* grow up around famous figures. That's just one way people have of saying, 'This was a truly remarkable person.' Patrick was a *real* man, though, and a brave one. Largely because of him, the Irish people became faithful Roman Catholic Christians, though their beliefs were rather different from those of the Pope in Rome.

"Which brings us back to Gregory, back to Rome," Dr. Jackson continued. "The story goes that one day Pope Gregory was down at the marketplace, where he saw some boys lined up in the slave market. They looked different, with their blond hair. 'Who are they?' asked the pope. 'They are Angles,' came the answer, 'from Angle-land.' 'Ah,' said Gregory, 'not Angles—but Angels!' Apparently the pope couldn't get those fair-haired slave boys out of his mind. So he made plans at once to send missionaries to Angle-land. He sent Augustine, who later became Bishop of Canterbury, and forty other monks to Christianize England."

Dr. Jackson handed Anna a charcoal pencil. "Here, Anna—why don't you draw in Gregory, Saint Patrick, and Augustine of England on our bridge, while I tell you about one more great missionary of those early days."

"Uh . . . I'll try," said Anna, and she began to draw while Dr. Jackson continued.

"Missionaries from Christian sections went to pagan sections, and in this way, Europe gradually became Christian. One missionary named Boniface went from England to Germany. Now, the Germans worshiped a god they called Wotan. There was a huge old oak tree which they believed was Wotan's holy place. Boniface said he would cut the whole tree down, which would prove that Wotan was not a god at all. The pagans all moved out of the way when Boniface picked up an ax. They were sure that Wotan would kill him with a lightning bolt. But the legend says that when Boniface struck the tree, it immediately broke into pieces. Then Boniface used the pieces to build one of the first Christian churches in Germany. Perhaps it was not just because the tree broke apart, but also because of the way Boniface lived, that made the people of that tribe want to become Christian. Later, the men of another German tribe killed Boniface.

"Missionaries moved all across the map, until at last the only pagans left were the Saxons, the toughest tribe of all. They had no use for missionaries or for any Christians. It took twenty-six years for Emperor Charlemagne of France to subdue the Saxons. When he did, he forced them all to be baptized in the river. But afterward, they went right back to their pagan life."

"Hmmmm," said Pam. "You mean, the Christian leaders made people become Christian even if they didn't want to?"

"Sometimes, yes. Of course, they didn't make people become *good* Christians that way. Later on, the Saxons became good Christians by their *own* choice."

Dr. Jackson reached over to add Boniface to the group on the bridge. "And now," he said, "by *our* own choice, let's call it a day."

"Okay! It's a day!" shouted Kristi and Pam together. Dr. Jackson joined in the laughter.

Jeff thought to himself, And it's a *good* day, at that.

Chapter 8

RECESS: BEING CHILDREN

The next afternoon, the five young people came skateboarding along the sidewalk that wound into the park. Jeff led the way, with Jason right behind him. Then came Anna, close on their heels. Pam and Kristi became tangled up trying to go backward and finally arrived carrying their skateboards. Nobody bumped into Saint Francis this time.

"Hi, friends," said Dr. Jackson. "I brought cookies and punch today, and I thought maybe we would do something different. History tells us about famous adults, but it never seems to say much about children, although the church has made an incredible difference in their lives. So now . . . just as we are about to get into the Middle Ages, let's take time out to talk about what the world back then was like for young people."

"Yeah," said Jason. "Let's hear it for the kids!" The others cheered their approval.

Dr. Jackson folded his long legs under him and sat on the grass with the half-circle of youngsters. "Well, young people in earlier times were much like you, but their *lives* certainly were quite different. To begin with, they did not have all the things most children have today. Many were often hungry and some even starved. Their houses—or huts—had only fireplaces

or open fires for heat. There were no water faucets or bathtubs. The toilet was a little house out back, or sometimes not even that."

"No TVs," mourned Kristi.

"No, no TV. But some things were not so different. Boys and girls in those days didn't have skateboards or bicycles, but they played catch, and jacks, and all sorts of race and relay games, and they did have toys—most of them the kind you can make yourself. And maybe that's the best kind. Girls had simple dolls, and boys made toy soldiers. In those days, children dressed as though they were small-sized adults. The very small children generally wore long robes. In warm countries, of course, many children didn't wear anything at all."

"I'd like that way best," said Pam impulsively. The others shushed her, but giggled their agreement.

"Most babies were wrapped up snugly in a *swaddling cloth*. That was a long strip of cloth which was wound around and around the little body, including arms and legs. The infant could scarcely move at all. So it was hard for babies to learn to use their arms and legs. But it was the custom, so no one thought to question it. Swaddling clothes were used for hundreds of years.

"One of the biggest differences between our time and theirs is in family life. Modern families sometimes have a problem because too few people live under one roof. Many of you know children who have only one parent at home. But in early times, there usually were both father and mother *plus* a number of aunts and uncles and cousins, as well as grandparents, all living together. That was nice, but crowded. And it created another sort of problem.

"In Roman times, children frequently were neglected and sometimes treated quite harshly. Many times parents who thought they had too many children would sell the extra ones to be slaves. Some unwanted babies were taken out in the country and thrown away. That was cruel of course, but people did it, and few objected until the church began to teach a better way—loving concern for all people."

Anna was troubled, her face sad. "But didn't anybody feel sorry for all those poor little kids?" she asked. "Dumped like that—without any food, and maybe in the cold winter!"

"Wow," said Kristi. "That was pretty mean."

"Yes," Dr. Jackson agreed, "it was. But you see, parents in some cultures didn't feel the same way toward their children that most people today feel. Many babies and young children died—and maybe the parents just couldn't let themselves love their children too deeply, because losing several would *hurt* them more than they could bear. Remember, too, that some of the parents were only children themselves. Yes, that's true. Parents arranged marriages for their children, and boys and girls of twelve were considered old enough to marry. Sometimes even younger girls were married—as young as you are, Pam and Kristi. There were no laws to protect children then. Both Greeks and Romans did with children just about anything they wanted. It was pretty sad."

Dr. Jackson stopped talking for a minute. Jeff was glad. He needed a bit of silence to sort all that out.

"And there wasn't much education," Dr. Jackson was going on. "That was part of the problem. Many people believed in magic, in evil spirits. For example, if a child were born 'different'—say, with too many or too few fingers—many people thought that it was the work of the devil. The child was regarded as a *changeling*, a demon in disguise. Such a child, many felt, should be killed. Sometimes even if a baby cried too much, it might be considered a changeling. It was not cruelty as much as ignorance . . . and fear. People didn't know any better." Dr. Jackson paused again, and then went on.

"Why do I tell you these sad things? Because it is part of the story. A sad part. But children did manage to grow up and live out their lives, in spite of everything. It's just that life was harder in those days. As more and more people became Christian, they began to change some things. The changes came slowly, but life became better when the church was there to help. Laws were passed to protect children. Church leaders taught that Christian parents should take good care of their children. They should have them baptized and teach them Christian ways. The church leaders reminded people that Jesus loved little children, that God wanted them protected and cared for. Gradually, things became more livable for children. For a long time, some people continued to abandon unwanted babies, though it was now against the law, and some children were sold into slavery. But Christians began to believe that if parents did not know how to take care of their children, or if they didn't care, then the church ought to take up that responsibility.

"An Italian bishop in Milan had a new idea. He said that the church should fix up a home for abandoned children. By this time people often left their extra, or unwanted, children on a church doorstep, rather than out in the country. 'What shall we *do* with these church-door babies, these *found-lings*?' the bishop asked. He answered his own question by establishing an orphanage, a foundlings' home."

"Oh, that's good!" cried Pam, relieved. The story had really been getting pretty sad.

Dr. Jackson went on, "As time went on, people began to understand children better, too. It was as if, for the first time, they could really *see* children. They discovered childhood. They began to realize that children are different from grown-ups. A child is not just a miniature, a model of his or her parents. Children are real people. They have feelings of their own—feelings about who they are, about their bodies, about being alive, about being somebody. And they need to be helped to feel good about themselves."

Once again the professor stopped talking, and again Jeff was grateful for the pause. The others, too, were quiet, thinking.

"So what I really want to say to you today is that you are a part of the story. You and children before you, all the way across that big bridge, from the time of Jesus to the present day, are part of the story. The figures we have drawn on the bridge are adults, but young people were there, too. And there's one thing I've noticed about young people," he added. "They grow up—and some of them become famous. Oh— and *all* of them are hungry! I say, Jeff, pass the cookies . . . and hand me that thermos of punch!"

Chapter 9

KINGS AND CRUSADES

It had rained a little the night before, and when Dr. Jackson and his young friends gathered in the park, the ground was still wet. The seats on one bench were driest—so Kristi and Pam and Jason crowded together on the seat, and Anna and Jeff sat on the back of the bench with their feet on the seat. Dr. Jackson half-sat on the pedestal of Saint Francis' statue.

"The next part of the story," he began, "is complicated. But it is exciting, too, because it is full of adventures and knights and great battles. I'll try to make it easy."

"How can you make something hard easy, Dr. Jack?" asked Pam.

"Well, at least I can *leave out* a few of the people involved. Many, many important people—kings and bishops—are in the story, but I will talk about only a few of them. Remember, this part of the story takes us over the long middle arch in the time bridge. And Christianity was spreading into many different countries, which means more people and names to remember. But today I will choose just one emperor, two popes, and two kings. Here are their names." Dr. Jackson unfolded a piece of paper on which he had lettered:

Emperor Henry IV
Pope Gregory VII
Pope Innocent III
King Philip II
King John

"You know what the numbers mean, I think. Popes and rulers with the same name were given numbers. Otherwise, we would never know *which* Gregory or *which* Henry we were talking about.

"Now, on with the story. Emperor Henry IV and Pope Gregory VII lived at the same time and are part of the same tale. The pope was head of the Roman Catholic Church in all of Europe. The emperor was head of what was called the Holy Roman Empire, which included most of Europe. This empire was not really united—it had lots of small sections, each with its own ruler. It was connected like a jigsaw puzzle, which meant that the emperor had trouble keeping all the pieces together. The pope controlled some of the pieces, which were ruled over by bishops. The pope and the emperor were each determined to be the more important ruler. Pope Gregory VII, to show that he was the most powerful, invited Emperor Henry IV to come across the Alps to one of the pope's castles, in Canossa, Italy, for a conference. But when Henry arrived, Pope Gregory wouldn't open the castle doors. He made Henry and his attendants stay out in the cold for three days, until he finally decided to invite him inside. Of course, that really made Henry look foolish. Everybody heard the story, and it even became a proverb. 'Going to Canossa' meant *losing,* or being laughed at."

Jeff chuckled, thoughtfully, aware of both the Pope's success and the way Henry must have felt.

Dr. Jackson continued, "Later on Henry got even.

He captured Rome and forced the Pope to leave. Imagine the *Pope* leaving *Rome,* the Papal City. The story certainly illustrates the way two strong rulers will fight for power. Neither side can win everything all the time. And that struggle went on through most of the Middle Ages. The popes said, 'We are leaders of God's Church; we are the most important rulers.' But the emperors and kings said, 'You rule the church; God has given the rule of the nations to us.'

"The next two names on our list illustrate the same situation, almost a hundred years later. While Pope Innocent III was the leader of the church, King Philip II of France divorced his queen and married another woman. He was king, and he thought that certainly gave him the right to do anything he wanted to do. But the Roman Catholic Church did not recognize divorce. And Pope Innocent said, 'Philip, you must take the queen back.' *And Philip did.* That's how powerful the Pope was.

"At about that same time, the church in England had chosen a new man to be the Archbishop of Canterbury. The English king, John, did not like the man they had chosen, so he appointed another leader for the church. But Pope Innocent in Rome said that kings couldn't do such things, and he forced John to accept the church's choice."

"What was King John's number?" asked Kristi.

"Glad you asked," said Dr. Jackson. "There was only one King John, so he didn't need a number. He was not a popular king, so young princes born afterward just weren't named for him."

"Oh, Dr. Jack," Pam interrupted. "If he was the only King John, then he's the one in the poem" . . . and she began to recite:

King John was not a good man—
He had his little ways.
And sometimes no one spoke to him
For days and days and days.

Dr. Jackson laughed. "He's the one, Pam. He taxed the people heavily, both to pay for his wars and to put the country on a more sound financial basis. Actually, he was sort of a bad character, but a pretty good administrator."

"Was he the Magna Carta John?" Jeff asked.

"Yes," Dr. Jackson explained, "he had done several things that the English people felt a king did not have the right to do. So the great knights and barons of England drew up the Magna Carta—which means the *big charter,* or the *great paper*—and they forced King John to sign it. Our American Bill of Rights in the Constitution is based on that list.

"Incidentally, Pope Innocent did not like that charter at all. But this time the pope lost. He couldn't fight a whole people. So the English kept their Great Charter."

"What about knights and battles, Dr. Jack?" pleaded Jason. "You promised us knights and battles."

"Absolutely," the professor said, and began at once on one of the most exciting stories of the Middle Ages. "While those five rulers were fighting about who would be head ruler in Europe, things were happening in Palestine. That was where Christianity began, back in the time of Jesus' earthly ministry. After the Roman Empire broke up, the eastern part of the Empire, with its headquarters in Constantinople, managed to survive for many more years. But then the Turks swept down from Asia. They captured Constantinople, Palestine and Jerusalem, and many other Christian holy places where Jesus had lived and taught. The Turks were *Moslems,* followers of the Arabian prophet called *Muhammad.* But Jerusalem was *their* holy place, too, and they claimed it with their swords. Instead of churches, they built *mosques* with high towers. Instead of steeples with bells, there were priests called *muezzins,* who climbed up the tall towers and called the people to prayer by blowing their horns. The Christians of Europe were shocked that the holy places of Christendom should be in the hands of infidels. 'We must *do* something,' they said. The pope told them what they should do: 'Go on a Crusade to rescue the holy places.' Many rulers and knights responded to his call. The word *crusade* comes from the word *cross.* It is a holy mission to rescue or defend the faith. Several great crusades were made to Palestine. Some were partly successful; others failed totally. Kings, emperors, dukes, barons, knights, and common soldiers went by the thousands. Many lost their lives far from home. But the pope said, 'A Crusader is like a holy pilgrim. To die on a Crusade is to die for Christ.' That's why some of them went. Others went because, after all, a crusade was a great adventure."

Jason broke in. "I suppose children were not allowed to go," he said bitterly. Boy Scout camping trips had given him a taste for adventure, and he would like to have gone on an adventurous crusade to far places.

"But they did!" exclaimed Jeff, and Dr. Jackson backed him up.

"Yes, here is the surprise, Jason. At first, not many children went. But there was one that was called the Children's Crusade. It was started by children, or by young teenagers, eager to rescue the holy city. And it was joined by many brave boys and girls who wanted to 'spend their lives for God.' A boy named Stephen went through France gathering children, and a boy named Nicholas collected an army of German children. They came by the thousands. Their fathers and mothers couldn't stop them. Many ran away from home to join Stephen and Nicholas.

"Well, the leaders were very young and not experienced in planning ahead. For awhile, the way to Jerusalem was fairly easy, and some adults helped them. They were on an adventure, and as they marched, they sang what we know as the Crusaders' Hymn:

> Fair are the meadows,
> Fairer still the woodlands,
> Robed in the the blooming garb of spring:
> Jesus is fairer, Jesus is purer,
> Who makes the woeful heart to sing.

"While the children were crossing the Alps to reach the sea, many died of starvation and cold. The rest made it into Italy, where they went first to Rome for the pope's blessing. He did bless them, but he urged them to go back home until they were grown. Some obeyed, but many continued on their journey.

"The French children, about five thousand of them, marched south and sailed for Palestine with some friendly sailors who offered to take them on their ships. They sailed away—and disappeared. Many years later, other crusaders found out that two of the ships had been wrecked. The rest never reached Palestine, because the friendly sailors were really slave dealers. All the children, boys and girls alike, many only ten or twelve years old, were sold in Africa as slaves. The sailors became rich. The children, many of them, remained good Christians, but they never saw Jerusalem. And they never saw their homes again."

"That's awful!" commented Anna. "I'd hate to go so far from home and end up a slave."

"Those leaders were no good," said Jason. He was disappointed. He wished that the story had turned out differently—that the children had freed Jerusalem.

Dr. Jackson could see his disappointment. He tried to explain. "Well, it was a poor plan from the start. The young people didn't know how to go about getting food and shelter. Adult crusaders had trouble planning those things for such masses of people. The youngsters had no money to back up their project. They had very few weapons. What they did have was an adventurous spirit and a great faith. They needed those. What they also needed was a plan other than *war* to focus their spirit and faith on."

"I'm sorry for all those kids," said Pam. "Just think, even I might have had a chance to go on a crusade." Jeff nodded his approval—and his agreement. Bravery was not something that had gone out with the Middle Ages.

"Nowadays," Dr. Jackson added, "there aren't any crusades to go on. But there are still lots of great adventures. Some of them are in foreign lands—in the mission field. Some of them are in new and unfamiliar places in our own land. Some of them are in tackling such enemies of the people of God as world hunger, poverty, loneliness, and war itself. Children can still find brave things to do for their church and for their faith. Really *following* Jesus is not an easy thing. And it can be the most exciting enterprise on earth!"

Chapter 10

THE AGE OF FAITH

It was Saturday, and the group had decided to meet at the playground area of the park, rather than around Francis' statue. It was a good playground. Besides the usual slides and swings, there was a corkscrew slide that spiraled down and around until it dumped you, dizzy, on the ground. There were three different kinds of jungle gyms made of shiny pipes and smooth logs. There were tunnels and little houses and parallel bars.

Pam was the star athlete of the group. Her strong brown arms and legs flashed as she did tricks on the parallel bars—tricks she had learned in gym class at school. Kristi and Anna laughed and giggled as they climbed like monkeys on the jungle gym and hung upside down. Jason made a swing go so high that the chains jumped and jerked. Even Jeff and Dr. Jackson joined in—swinging and playing like the rest.

But half an hour of such vigorous play is tiring—by then they *all* were out of breath. Dr. Jackson found a quiet cool corner of the playground and sat on the thick grass to rest. The others, one by one, joined him, ready for the story to continue.

"We have tried to imagine what life was like a thousand years ago, but it is hard to do, because it was so different," Dr. Jackson began. "The century from 1200 to 1300 has sometimes been called the Great Age of Faith. The church and the pope were strong; cathedrals soared; monasteries flourished. And thoughts about God and human life became important. The most famous thinker and writer was Thomas Aquinas, who entered the University of Naples at the age of fifteen.

"At that time, educated people still were influenced by ancient Greek and Roman thinking about life. Christian thinkers like Thomas, who became a Dominican monk, believed that God taught truth in the Bible and in the church and also in the lives of people. So he brought together all those sources of knowledge and found that they agreed. There is, he said, a world of nature that we can study, too. All is from God. World-knowledge and faith-knowledge will always agree. Thomas wrote huge books that are still studied by people called Thomists.

"Although there is a lot that is different now, there is also a lot that is pretty much the same. Maybe it will help if we talk about the church of those times—in some ways it was not so different from the church today. For instance, we still use the same Bible to learn about God. And church buildings are not so different now, either. Churches are usually built to last a long time, and some of the churches built in the Middle Ages are still used today. There is Canterbury Cathedral in England, and Notre Dame (which means *Our Lady*) in Paris is another very old cathedral. There is also one in Mainz, Germany. Those three cathedrals are of *Gothic* architecture. Do you have a mental picture of what Gothic churches look like?"

Pam responded, "We had a film in school about old castles and churches. And I thought the churches looked like the castles. They were so strong, and the walls were so thick."

Dr. Jackson agreed. "Some churches *were* like forts or castles. And deliberately so, because sometimes the priests and monks and people had to defend their churches against enemies. That is one reason they were built that way. But there was another reason. Jeff, you're the architect. Any good guesses?"

"Sure," said Jeff. "Strong walls were the only way they could hold the roof up."

"Right. And a third reason was that they wanted their churches to last forever. Do you remember anything else about the way they looked, besides the thick walls?"

"Well," Pam said, "they were high, with towers or spires. Some had little windows and some had really big ones."

"Yes. The oldest chuches had small windows. Later, the builders discovered ways to brace the high walls so that they could have bigger openings for windows. The braces were called *buttresses*—like this . . ." and Dr. Jackson laid twigs on the ground to show walls and buttresses. "Some buttresses were set up some distance from the walls and connected to them only at the top. Those are called *flying* buttresses. The builders tried hard to discover a way to build big churches without too many pillars inside to hold the ceiling up. Remember, they didn't have steel girders then.

"Usually the floor plan of the Gothic church was in the shape of a huge cross. You could see that, if you were a bird—or today, if you were in an airplane. The long part of the cross was called the *nave*. Far down at the end was the *altar*. With fine decorations and candles. That is where the priest said *mass*.

"Churches were almost always in the best location—right in the center of the town. People came to the church, to the center, from all directions, to hear the mass. They *heard* it, but they didn't *understand* much of it. That was because the service was read in Latin. The Romans had used Latin, but by this time, almost everyone had forgotten the language except the leaders of the church. Only the priest could say mass, because he was the only ordained minister, and because he was the only one who knew Latin. The church taught that, during the *sacrament* of the Mass, as the priest was holding the bread and wine, they truly became the body and blood of Christ. The Roman Catholic Church and the Eastern Orthodox Church still believe that this is the correct understanding of the Lord's Supper. Protestant churches teach that the bread and wine *represent* Christ's body and blood; but all the churches believe that the Lord's Supper is a true sacrament. The Bible tells us that Jesus himself taught his followers to worship together in a memorial supper."

Anna wanted to know, "What's a sacrament?"

Dr. Jackson explained: "It was in the Middle Ages that the church began to teach about sacraments. A sacrament is a 'channel of grace.' That means that through certain acts, the church can call the blessing of God upon the worshipers. The people become better Christians and can live closer to God's way because God's blessing purifies them. Their sins are forgiven. In the Middle Ages, when the Catholic Church was the *only* church, it was believed that the sacraments *automatically* cancelled out one's sins. Later on, during the Reformation, when other churches were formed, they taught that the sacraments would work only if both the minister and the people were well prepared and serious. But in the

Middle Ages, many believed that just being present was enough. Grace would flow from the sacraments like water from a faucet.

"There were seven sacraments. The Lord's Supper, or *Communion,* was one. *Baptism* was another. This sacrament was for everyone, even new babies. Baptism showed that a baby was already under God's care. This would protect the infant against all sorts of evils, including bad spirits, gremlins, witches, bogey men, and elves."

Anna giggled. Jeff grinned. Kristi nodded. She was always interested in elves and fairies and other little people of the forest. Most of them were very nice, but some. . . . "You mean, in the church the bad goblins couldn't get you?" she asked.

"That's what people believed then. After baptism came *confirmation,* for children old enough to make promises of membership. The Lord's Supper, or Mass, was to keep the faith strong all through life. Then there was the sacrament of *penance.* That was something people said or did to make up for their sins. After they confessed to a priest the wrong things they had said or done or thought, the priest could say that their sins were forgiven. Then he would tell them to do something to make up for their sins. They might be told to say a certain prayer a hundred times, or give money for a new church, or practice being kind to their fathers and mothers.

"The sacrament for people who were dying was called *extreme unction.* The sacrament of *marriage* was for men and women who wanted to marry and raise families. *Ordination* was to make people priests. That makes seven altogether. Catholic Churches still have seven sacraments. Many Protestants say that there are only two, because the New Testament records only two that were performed by Jesus. They feel that those two, baptism and Communion, are channels of grace. The rest are good ceremonies, but not sacraments.

"One of the big jobs of the church was teaching the people about Christianity. There were very few schools, and few people could go to those there were. Most ordinary people did not know how to read or write. How, then, could the churches teach the people about the faith?"

Pam had her hand up. "They made lots of pictures, so people who could not read could *see* the Christian story."

"Right. All those wonderful pictures and statues and stained-glass windows were 'the Bible of the people.' Through them, they could learn the story of Joseph and his brothers in Egypt. They could *see* Jesus teaching the people and healing the sick. They could *see* the sad story of the crucifixion and the happy story of Easter. Some of the pictures were painted on plaster walls that did not last. Others were mosaics, made of fine pieces of colored stone or glass. There were statues carved of wood, molded in clay, or chipped out of marble, like our statue of Francis. The stained-glass windows were pictures, too, filled with important lessons from the Bible.

"Besides all these, there were fine manuscript books. We still haven't come to the printing press, so those books were lettered by hand. Imagine the work involved in hand printing a whole big book! One of the most famous books of that time was Dante's *Divine Comedy*. The word *comedy* doesn't mean that it was a *funny* book; it just means that in the end, everything turned out all right. Dante told that one day when he was lost in a great forest, three wild beasts frightened him, but a stranger appeared and drove the animals away. The stranger was Virgil, a Roman poet who really had lived about the time of Jesus. Then Virgil became Dante's guide, and took him to a great opening in the ground. Down there, he explained, was hell, or the inferno. And he offered to take Dante on a guided tour. Dante wasn't sure he wanted to go down to that scary place. But Virgil showed him the way.

"Remember, now, that Dante was describing an imaginary trip. He told of seeing sinners living in everlasting punishment. Then he described going with Virgil through the in-between land of *Purgatory*. There the people who had not been such terrible sinners were cleansed, so that they could go on to heaven.

"Now, Virgil had been a very fine and wise man. But since he had not known about Christianity, he was a pagan, and in the story, he could not be Dante's guide to heaven. His place was taken by a beautiful Christian girl named Beatrice. She showed Dante all the wonders, even where the King of Peace (Jesus) and the Queen of Heaven reigned.

"Well, Dante's book illustrates how people of the Middle ages thought of the world. They believed it had three layers, like a big cake. In the middle was a flat earth, underneath was hell, and heaven was in the sky. With the help of the sacraments, people felt they had a chance to end up in heaven instead of in hell.

"So everybody crowded into the beautiful churches. The services were rich and wonderful. Organs were invented. Hymns were composed and sung. One of the oldest begins:

> Come, Holy Ghost, our souls inspire,
> And lighten with celestial fire.

"Perhaps the most famous of all was the 'Te Deum Laudamas,' which is Latin for 'We Praise You, O God.'

> We praise thee, O God;
> we acknowledge thee to be the Lord.
> All the earth doth worship thee,
> the Father everlasting . . .

That's the way it begins."

Jason broke in. "That kind of worship seems too serious. I don't think I'd like it. And who wants to listen to a lot of Latin?"

Dr. Jackson replied, "That's the response of the twentieth century, Jason. But you wouldn't have felt that way if you had lived way back in those days. Life was hard for almost everyone, even rich people. There were many dangers, both from nature and from other people. A reasonably healthy young man could expect to live to be, maybe, thirty-five. And besides all the *real* perils of plagues and wars, people imagined some even worse: goblins and evil spirits. A person could never tell when one of those might be around. And even if they never came, a person still lived in fear that they might. Worst of all was God's judgment on sinners.

"So the church helped people feel safer, with its services of worship and with the sacraments. In the church, at least, good was stronger than evil. Only in the church, people felt, could they be true Christians and be saved. It *was* serious worship, Jason. 'Serious' was close to the lives of the people. And the church meant much to them. That is one reason we call that time the Age of Faith."

Chapter 11

IT'S EASY TO SLIDE DOWNHILL

A week had gone by—longer than usual between times of talking about the people on the bridge of church history. But Dr. Jackson had been out of town. Now he was back—and it was a sunny Sunday afternoon—and he and his young friends met again at the park.

It's good to be together, Jeff thought.

"It's good to be together again," Dr. Jackson began, and he wondered why Jeff grinned. He went on, "Today we are going to talk about sliding downhill."

"Hooray!" cried Kristi. "I know how you can slide downhill, without a sled, even—or snow. All you need is a big box—you know, like for groceries."

Jason said, "How's this?" and he pulled a shallow box out of a trash can.

"Oh, that's perfect," said Kristi, and she looked around. Close by was a small but rather steep hill with thick unmowed grass. The long grass was straw-colored. "Watch—I'll show you!"

While the others looked on, Kristi scrambled up the hill. She plopped down on the box and drew up her knees so that her feet were on the box, too. Then she pushed off with her hands. The smooth box slid on the slick grass, and down she came. On the way, the box twisted around, so that at the bottom she was

backward and tumbled off, rolling in the grass. Kristi hopped up, brushed off, and handed the box to Jason. "Try it," she said. "It's fun!"

So Jason did. And then Anna, and Pam, and even Jeff. When he got to the bottom, he looked around at Dr. Jackson. "Want a turn?" he asked.

The professor grinned, took the nearly worn-out box back up the hill and had his own fast ride. Then he tossed the box back into the trash, took time to catch his breath, and began to talk.

"Your game is a perfect beginning for our story today, Kristi. You see, we are going to talk about how the church can slide downhill, just like we did. Only it's not as much fun. It is a sad thing to see churches, and the Christians in them, go downhill. I think you know what I mean. Churches sometimes grow and progress, but sometimes they stop growing. Sometimes they even become stagnant, or stale. This is the point in our story of the bridge when the church quite definitely became stagnant.

"The church had been around a long time. We are talking about the 1200s to 1400s. There are a lot of people on the bridge now, for the church had grown very large. And it had become rich. It owned lands, and ran farms, and had much business to attend to. What happened in the church also sometimes happens in families. If the father and mother have important things to do that keep them always busy, and if the children are always off to some school or sport or Scout meeting, they are not together often as a family. It is easy for them to forget how much they love one another.

"That's partly what happened in the church. The leaders had so many other things to do that they sometimes forgot what the church was for—to follow Jesus and to care for people. And some bad habits had crept into the church. There were some selfish, and greedy, and even cruel leaders. The church was going downhill, just as we did on the box. It's easy, you know.

"The popes, who were leaders of the Roman Catholic Church, had political troubles, too. For a number of years, they could not even live in Rome. Now, Rome was the capital city of the church—but political pressures had pushed the religious leaders out of their own city. They had to set up a temporary capital in a castle in southern France—a place called Avignon.

"In time, the pope returned to Rome, but then conditions became even worse. A great argument arose over which of two church leaders was the *real* pope. Unable to agree, they carried on for several years with *two* popes—one living in Rome and the other in Avignon. Christians felt bad about all this . . . even their leaders could not get along. They felt bad when one pope spent all his time leading his troops into war. Hmmm. Troops . . . the pope's army—sounds like some sort of Christian contradiction, doesn't it? In the midst of all this, some of the priests and bishops became rich . . . *too* rich. They were no longer interested in serving the churches. Instead, they wanted to be great rulers, like the princes and kings. It was a very sad state of affairs."

Anna broke in. "Was *everybody* bad? Weren't there *some* good people left in the church?"

"Of course. There were *many* good people in the church. But just a few bad ones will make the whole thing look bad. On the playground, one or two who are being obnoxious can spoil the game for everybody. Right?"

Jeff nodded and thought to himself, Sometimes I've been the spoiler.

Dr. Jackson continued. "Many people kept trying to lead Christian lives the best way they could, but frequently the church hurt them more than it helped. Remember, though, that all through the Middle Ages, there were smaller groups of Christians different from the two big churches, the Roman Catholic and the Eastern Orthodox. Most of those small groups were illegal. The law said that only the big official church could exist. But the little groups of Christians worshiped together anyway, sometimes secretly. They tried to live simply and honestly, and they believed they were closer to Jesus' way. Sometimes it was dangerous, and they had to leave the country or hide in the forests or mountains. If they were caught, they were jailed and sometimes even killed."

"I'd belong to one of those," said Jason firmly. There was something about danger that whetted his appetite.

"One of those little groups was called the Waldenses. They were followers of a Frenchman, Valdes, who later was sometimes called Peter Waldo. Valdes was not a priest, but a lay preacher and leader. The Waldenses kept their separate church all through the Middle Ages. Some of their churches are still active—about seventy in Italy, and a few in the United States and in South America.

"In Holland were the Brothers of the Common Life, a peaceful people who believed that the church should not be so great and rich. They believed in humility, simple living, and Christian love. A group like that is not as likely to slide downhill as a powerful, wealthy church. They set a good example, both with their lives and with their worship."

"I should think some of the folks in the *big* church would want to rebel," said Anna. "A greedy church

79

sure ought to make *some* of its members feel uncomfortable."

"You're right, Anna. Some of the leaders in the big church *did* want to make some changes. They were called Reformers. They wanted new rules, better ways to do things, and new leaders to guide them. One such Reformer was John Wyclif, an Englishman. He wanted the church to be more Christian, to follow the Bible more closely. But there were not many Bibles to follow."

"How come?" Kristi wanted to know.

"Who can answer that one?" asked Dr. Jackson.

"Well," said Jason, "back to the manuscript you were talking about the other day. Are we still before the printing press? Because if we are, they couldn't print books—they could only copy them. And that's *slow*."

"That's right, Jason. Of course they could make wood prints. They carved a picture or a page on a piece of wood, then covered it with ink and printed the picture. But that was about as hard and slow as lettering books by hand.

"So Wyclif could not print Bibles. But he did do something tremendously important. He and some helpers translated the Bible into English, the language of the people—in his country. Remember that Jerome, a long time ago, had put the Bible into Latin, because that was the language of the people then. But people didn't speak Latin any more. Would you know what I meant if I were the priest and began to read the morning Scripture to you . . . and it went like this?

> *Dominus regit me, et nihil mihi deerit;*
> *In loco pascuae ibi me collocavit*
> *Super aquam refectioniis educavit me. . . .*

That's all of it I remember."

"Whew!" said Jeff. "That's Greek to me!"

"Well," laughed Dr. Jackson, "it's *Latin*—the beginning of the Twenty-third Psalm."

"Humph!" said Kristi. "Don't see how it would do us any good to hear it, if we couldn't understand a word you were saying."

"Precisely," said Dr. Jackson. "That's why Wyclif's work was so important. He and his fellow workers copied his translation laboriously, with quill pens and ink.

"Then there was Erasmus. He was a very wise man—he was a native of Holland, though he lived all over Europe. He, too, was a good student of the Bible and a good writer. Because he cared about the church and wanted it to change and improve, he made jokes about it—about the bad leaders, hoping to make them reform. He told funny stories about rich priests and lazy monks and fat bishops. The people liked what he said and wrote. Erasmus hated war and loved peace. He was one of those who prodded on the later Reformers.

"Those leaders—Wyclif and Erasmus and others like them—did what they could. But the church kept on sliding downhill. Finally, by the end of the Middle Ages, other Reformers appeared. They insisted the church *must* be reformed, no matter what. They were willing to fight for what they believed was true Christianity. They were the leaders of what we call the Protestant Reformation. And they are the people whose big changes bring us from the Middle Ages into Modern Times."

Jason said, "We're Lutheran. Our church came from the Reformation."

Pam added, "And I'm a United Methodist. We are protestors, or Protestants, too."

"Yes, all the Protestant churches, one way or another, came from the time of the Reformation. We'll get to that tomorrow."

"Then how about another picnic?" suggested Anna. "If we are at the end of an arch on our bridge, we ought to celebrate!"

They all agreed.

Chapter 12

LUTHER GOES TO A PICNIC

The young people arrived early, in a mood of expectation. Not only was today picnic day, but their parents were going to join them during the last part of their class in the park. Jeff thought back to that first day when Pam had accused Saint Francis of tripping her. It's been a good *trip,* he thought and smiled at his own private joke.

Dr. Jackson arrived with a bit of a skip in his step, as if he were a little excited, too. "Is the picnic still on?" he asked.

"Yes!" "You bet!" "For sure!" chorused the group.

"Great," he said. "It will be a good day for a celebration, for getting across the big middle arch on our bridge. But first, I brought something to show you. It's a statue of the man who will stand right over the pillar where the middle arch ends and the last one begins." He handed Jeff a bronze statue, almost a foot tall and rather heavy. "Know who that is?" he asked.

Jeff looked at the sculpture. The figure was sturdy and strong, clothed in long thick robes. "Martin Luther, I think," Jeff guessed. "He's the only one I know who had anything to do with the Reformation."

"Right, Jeff. Luther is the most important of the Reformers, though there were several others. This is a copy of a giant statue in the city of Worms,

Germany. It is part of a group of statues made over a hundred years ago, in memory of the Diet of Worms (Dē-it of Vorms). Who knows what the Diet of Worms was?"

Jeff said, "Well, I have read in the enclyclopedia about a kind of government called a *diet*. It's sort of like our Congress."

"That's exactly right, Jeff. We are really talking about an important meeting of rulers, or a *diet*, which happened to be held in the city of Worms. This statue reminds us of that important meeting, more than four hundred fifty years ago. It was in that town of Worms, along the Rhine River, that Martin Luther made a brave speech. 'Here I stand,' he said, 'I can do no other.' "

"Was he a soldier in a war?" Pam wanted to know.

"Yes, Pam, but not the way you might think. His war was against evil in the church. He used words instead of swords. He wanted the church to become more Christian, the way it had been in Jesus' time. That is why he is called a Reformer. And that is why that movement is called the Reformation."

Jason had a question. "When did people first hear about Luther? Was it at the Diet of Worms?"

"No, Luther was already well known then, Jason. But let's go back to his youth: Once he happened to be out in a violent thunderstorm—and he was terrified. He was afraid not only of the thunder and lightning; he was also afraid that evil spirits were after him. Out of his fright, he called to St. Anne for help. 'St. Anne,' he cried. 'Save me! If you will save my life now, I will become a monk.' He said this as a vow . . . a promise. And of course you are not supposed to go back on a promise. The storm stopped, and Martin was safe. But now he felt that he really should enter a monastery.

"Luther spent several years as a monk. Life was hard in the monastery. But life had been hard at home, too. Martin's mother was superstitious; she feared evil spirits and goblins. His father was very strict and sometimes had punished Martin severely. But his home life had had its warm spots, too. His parents cared about him. He even learned to sing and to play the lute, which is somewhat like a guitar.

"Young Martin Luther went to school just as other young people did. Teachers, too, in those days were strict. There were two parts to the lesson—memorizing it perfectly, and being switched if you hadn't. At home Martin was punished when he did not behave; at school he was punished when he did not learn. And in the monastery, he was punished when he did not follow the rules. He even punished himself for not being good enough. He did this by not eating and by keeping night vigils, standing up all night long. He almost lost his health that way."

Anna asked, "But didn't he know he should take care of himself? Even children know they ought to eat right and keep their bodies healthy."

"That is what his leader in the monastery told him. 'Nobody can be perfect,' he said, 'even a monk. So it is foolish to punish yourself for not being perfect.' But Martin couldn't understand that. He felt he had to be perfect in order to *deserve* God's blessing. Finally, his life was saved through his discovery of a verse in the book of Romans. There he read, 'He shall gain life who is justified through faith' (1:17 NEB). To young Martin this seemed to be a personal message from God. You can't earn God's love. It's a gift. You can't make friends with God just by being good all the time. None of us can manage to be perfect. We are sort of like the little girl in the nursery rhyme.

> There was a little girl who had a little curl
> Right in the middle of her forehead.
> When she was good, she was very, very good,
> But when she was bad, she was horrid."

"Yes," said Kristi softly, remembering the lying-about-the-broken-vase episode at home last week.

"Luther continued to read the Bible with this new insight. He learned that just being sorry doesn't make everything right. He learned that the only way to achieve a right relationship with God is to let God do it. This is what belief in *Jesus* is all about. *He* came to show us what God is like and how God can give us faith. That is what makes things right, not anything we ourselves can do. Even if we keep on being 'horrid,' God still loves us."

"Hey!" shouted Pam suddenly. "There's my mother. And my father! Here comes the picnic!"

Pam's parents, then Kristi's, then the boys' mother, and Anna's, came sauntering up to the favorite spot by Francis' statue. The young people ran to help with thermos jugs and picnic baskets; Jason and Anna spread out a blanket. Soon those who had not met were doing so, and cheerful chatter filled the late afternoon. The food was spread out for all to enjoy. And by the time it was gone, the professor had become "Dr. Jack" to the parents, too. The young people tried to "catch the parents up" on the story of the bridge—and some of the parents discovered that the boys and girls already knew more about the history of the Christian church than *they* did.

Chapter 13

FIX-UP TIME

Three days had gone by. They were back at the park again, settling down on the grass. Jeff looked up at the statue with affection. Saint Francis and his birds and animals seemed a part of the group.

"We are on the last arch of our bridge now," Dr. Jackson began. "But traveling over *this* arch will take longer. Any guess why?"

"No," said Anna. "The middle arch is the longest time span. We have already come from the first century to the fifteenth, and that is three-fourths of the way to now. So why does the third arch take longer?"

"More complicated?" Jeff guessed.

"Yes, because it is much more crowded," said Dr. Jackson. "There are different kinds of churches in many different countries. We will need to take our time here, or it will just be a blur of people—and that's no fun.

"Remember that we are into the Protestant Reformation now. If we had our sketch of the bridge, we could draw in Martin Luther right over the stone pillar that holds up the two arches. Do any of you know what it was that made Martin Luther most famous?"

"I know, Dr. Jack," said Jason. "One day he went

up to the church in the town where he lived and tacked up a paper on the church door. We learned about that in Bible school."

"That is exactly what he did. And it was no ordinary paper. It was called the Ninety-five Theses. What do you suppose that means?"

"Almost a hundred of *something*," said Kristi. "Sounds like a list."

"Right! It was a list of ideas that Luther was challenging the church leaders to debate with him. He said that some of the teachings of the church needed to be examined. Most important to him right then were the teachings about doing good, to make up for doing bad. As we have seen, he had discovered in Paul's letters that that is not how it works. We don't *earn* the right to God's love and grace. We don't earn faith. Faith is a gift from God.

"Well, you know what happens when someone tries to change the old ideas and rules. Luther's Ninety-five Theses were questioning the teachings of the church. The church leaders were very angry. Some wanted to argue the ninety-five points. Others just wanted to punish him for daring to question the authorities. One way or another, Luther was in for a big fight.

"In fact, for most of the rest of his life, Luther was in big fights and little fights. Not with his fists, of course, but with words and ideas. He made speeches. He preached sermons. He wrote letters. He wrote little pamphlets. He wrote big books. With all these, he fought for what he was sure was true Christianity. He wanted the church to measure itself and judge itself by the teachings in the Bible. Luther felt that the pope himself was wrong . . . and would have to change."

Dr. Jackson paused, and Pam said, "I bet the pope didn't care much for that."

"Right, Pam. The pope was a powerful figure—and he wasn't about to let some ordinary priest upset his way of doing things. So he *excommunicated* Luther. This meant he put him out of the church. He could not go to the church for Mass and other sacraments. But in Wittenberg, where Luther lived, the other priests allowed him to come to church. And the ruler of that area defended him.

"Germany was being divided into two parts: those *for* Luther and those against him. Luther had not wanted that. He had hoped the whole church would reform. But Germany divided, and the part opposed to Luther remained Catholic. Those who followed Luther's reforms took his name and called themselves. . . ."

"Lutherans!" said Kristi.

"Correct. While this was going on, the emperor called that great meeting we talked about, the Diet of Worms. There Luther was told that he would have to obey the pope of the church. He tried to explain his feelings, and then he made that famous statement, 'Here I stand; God help me, I can do no other.' Well, both the pope and the emperor would now be against him. But Luther was able to leave the meeting a free man because the emperor had promised him safe passage.

"Luther left Worms with one close friend. But he kept looking over his shoulder as he went out of the city. He knew he was in danger. Suddenly, when he was near his own birthplace on the way back to Wittenberg, a group of armed men sprang out of the woods. A couple of them grabbed the reins of his horse. Then they took Luther and rode off into the forest. He had been kidnapped! He simply disappeared! Some people thought he was dead. Others thought he probably was in one of the emperor's dungeons."

"Oh, golly," cried Kristi. "Then what?"

"Well, many nobles supported Luther, and his friends had feared for his life. After awhile, a rumor began to spread: 'Luther is safe with his friends in a secret place.' This turned out to be true! One of Luther's supporters, a great ruler, had planned to get him out of the way for his own safety. So . . . he really *was* kidnapped—but by his own friends. He was taken to a remote castle called Wartburg, where he would be safe until 'the heat was off.' He even had a disguise—a beard—and a new name. Those who took food to him knew him only as Sir George, a knight.

"Luther used that time at the castle to do some important writing. Later when it was safe, he came back to Wittenberg. And there he began to make the changes in the church that he felt were needed. He changed the Catholic Mass into the simpler Lutheran Lord's Supper. Luther felt that the consecrated bread and wine *were* the body and blood of Christ, because Christ was there along with the bread and wine. However, this was not something done by the priest, but rather by the grace of God. Only Christians who were prepared and sincere could benefit from the Communion. Just being there to hear the priest say the mass in Latin was not enough.

"There were other reforms. Luther insisted that a worship service should always include readings from the Bible. The preacher should always preach a sermon based on the Bible lessons. All the people should be taught to sing hymns. One of the hymns Luther himself wrote is still sung in many churches, especially on Reformation Sunday in the fall," and Dr. Jack began to sing . . .

> A mighty fortress is Our God,
> A bulwark never failing;
> Our helper he amid the flood
> Of mortal ills prevailing.

"You know another song that Luther sang, though he may not have written it." Dr. Jackson began, and the children joined in:

> Away in a manger,
> No crib for a bed,
> The Little Lord Jesus laid down his sweet head.
> The stars in the sky looked down where he lay,
> The little Lord Jesus, asleep on the hay.

"Luther also insisted on some reforms for the clergy. Monks and nuns, he felt, should leave the monasteries and live like other people in the towns and cities. They should marry and raise families. They should live *among* the people."

"Like preachers do today," said Pam.

Dr. Jackson continued, "Well, all these changes brought Luther a lot of trouble. In those days artists made woodcuts . . . we have talked about those . . . pictures or words carved on wooden blocks so they could be printed. Some of them looked rather like modern comic strips. Catholics drew cartoons of Luther as a seven-headed monster. Protestants drew cartoons of the pope with a broken key, his hat falling off. Some of the cartoons were pretty vicious. All this made people on both sides very angry. Finally they actually went to war. Catholic Christians and Protestant Christians in Germany were killing one another in battle. That was really sad. For Luther, too. He had wanted to repair the church, not divide it."

Anna remarked, "Grown-ups act worse than kids, sometimes. Even if they were sorry about it afterward, it wouldn't help. People would already have been killed."

"That's right, Anna. The Reformation made many important changes, though it is too bad the changes could not have been made in an easier way. But the Reformation made life much better, especially for women and girls. Remember that when little girls were not wanted, they were sold or given away? Well, the Reformation stopped much of that. Women still were not treated equally, but family life improved.

"Luther was a family man and loved his children. But in his large family, the noise of children running and playing sometimes bothered him when he was trying to study. And one time he thoughtlessly cut a big piece out of his son Hans' pants to patch his own. He *loved* his family, though—his wife, Katey (whom he sometimes called Katey-my-rib), and Hans, and his daughters, too. When one of the little girls, Magdalena, became ill and died, he was very, very sad. To Luther, family life was an ideal, even better than the *celibate,* or solitary, life of single priests and monks and nuns. 'God,' said Luther and the other Reformers, 'should be worshiped in the world, in the midst of everyday life.'

"Enough for now," Dr. Jackson interrupted himself. "Luther's reform began the Protestant Reformation. Out of it came a number of churches: Lutheran, Presbyterian, Episcopalian, Congregational, Mennonite. Next time we will find out about those and others . . . and talk about why there are so many different kinds of churches."

Chapter 14

MORE FIXING UP

The group had agreed that when it rained, they would meet at Dr. Jackson's house. So on this particular day, Pam and Kristi, and then Anna, ran through the downpour to Dr. Jackson's front door. The two boys were the last to arrive, and when they were all inside and settled on the floor, Dr. Jackson started right in.

"Martin Luther was the most famous of the Reformers," he said, "but he didn't accomplish the Reformation all by himself. He led the reform of the church in Germany, which was very important. Luther was very strong and brave, and very smart. But he had a bit of a temper! Sometimes he called people who disagreed with him bad names, and he argued with people who wanted to reform the church in a different way. But people who did not live in Germany and did not even speak his language did not particularly feel like following this German. The need for change was obvious to many people, but the Reformation came to different countries in different ways."

"People in different countries are *different*," Jason said.

"True," agreed Dr. Jackson. "Certainly different churches appeal to different sorts of people. Some suit those who like a fine service in a beautiful temple, with music and organs. Other churches suit people who want simple worship in plain meeting houses, with only their own voices for music. Some like ritual, written down in books. Others want lively gospel songs and guitars. Still others want good preaching most of all. There are even some who worship best just sitting quietly together, doing nothing at all. They believe that this gives *God* a chance to do something. All these are genuine ways for Christian people to worship.

"So it makes sense that there would be room for other kinds of reform besides Luther's. Two of the most important began in the little country of Switzerland. A man named *Zwingli* lived in *Zurich*. Two Zs. That might help you remember him. He became a Reformer about the same time as Luther, and for some of the same reasons. Like Luther, he felt the church had fallen into bad ways. He said that the pope had stolen the keys of the Kingdom from Saint Peter. A woodcut cartoon came out shortly after that, showing Saint Peter wrestling with the pope, trying to get the keys back!

"Two things, it seems to me, are important about Zwingli. One is biblical preaching. Remember, now, that people didn't have their *own* Bibles. And the priests read only selected passages from the Scriptures, and only in Latin. So when Zwingli started preaching from the New Testament, beginning with Matthew 1:1, and taking verse by verse each Sunday until he had gone all the way through, people were excited! They were hearing every single verse of the Bible!"

"Gee," said Anna. "We sure take a lot for granted, don't we?"

Dr. Jackson nodded. "Actually, parts of the Bible had not been known by the people for over a

thousand years! No wonder they were excited about hearing it! One listener said it made the hair stand up on his head.

"Zwingli, like Luther, said that the Bible should be the guide for Christian life and worship. But here is the difference: Luther said that if a custom is not forbidden in the Bible, it is all right to do it. Zwingli said that unless the Bible commands it, it is forbidden. For example, the Bible has nothing to say about stained-glass windows. Therefore, Luther said, they were permitted. But Zwingli said they were forbidden, because nowhere does the Bible say that churches *should* have stained-glass windows. For this reason, all the stained-glass windows in Zurich were taken out or broken. But in Wittenburg, Luther's town, they were left in place.

"In Zurich, they took out organs, too, and removed the statues of the saints. If you visit Zurich today, you can still see the great cathedral, one of the places where Zwingli preached. Around the outside you will see many headless statues on the walls. Some Reformers had knocked off their heads—except for the ones that were too high to reach."

Kristi interrupted. "I think that's awful. I'll bet some of those statues and windows were beautiful. Dr. Jack, how could they be so mean?"

"Hard question, Kristi," said Dr. Jackson. "I can only partly answer it. In those days, Christians were very serious about their faith. We should be (and some people are) as serious about it today. But in Zwingli's time, when the people first realized that they themselves could use the Bible as a guide . . . breaking away from the idea that the priests did all the thinking and told them what they should believe and how they were to act . . . well, that was so exciting that some people were carried away. We all like to be challenged, and they saw a 'return to the Bible' Christianity as God's own challenge to them. Later on, they relaxed a little and no longer did those violent things like breaking windows and statues."

Jason said, "Some people act like that today. They get an idea, and they think everyone should agree. Uh . . . *fanatic*—that's the word for it."

"Yes, Jason. A fanatic," said Dr. Jackson to Pam's questioning look, "is someone who does so much of one thing, or makes so much of one idea, that he or she can't think much else. And as we see, there were some religious fanatics in Reformation times, just as there always have been. Just as there still are. Luther was not a fanatic; neither, really, was Zwingli. But Zwingli, like Luther, had strong ideas. He thought Luther did not complete his reform work. So you might say he reformed the Reformer.

"Both of them believed in the Bible as the guide for the church. But they differed, as people still do, on what the Bible means. For instance Luther read that Jesus took bread at the Last Supper and told his disciples, 'This is my body.' 'The Bible says so, the Bible means so,' said Luther. 'The bread *is* Jesus' body because Jesus is there along with the bread.' Zwingli read the same passage, and he said, 'Jesus meant that the bread *stands for*, or represents, his body, but the bread is just bread.' He went on to point out that when Jesus said 'I am the true vine,' he was not calling himself part of a tree."

"These things are hard for even adults to under-stand, which is another reason there were different kinds of Reformation. People had, and have today, honest differences about what some parts of the Bible mean. By the twentieth century, we have pretty well learned how to be Christian friends, even though we do have differences in belief. In some ways our differences are good. They give Christians the choices we talked about."

"You said two Reformers came from Switzerland, Dr. Jack. Who was the other one?" Jeff asked.

"John Calvin. Actually, he *came* from France, but he started his reform movement in Switzerland. It was dangerous to be a Reformer in France. One would very likely be put in jail. John Calvin came from a poor family, but he managed to get a good education in Paris. He was so bright that he entered the university when he was only fourteen. He read some of Luther's sermons and some of the writings of Erasmus and Zwingli—and he agreed with them. He also had some ideas of his own about church reform.

"Calvin decided to leave France, so he went to Geneva, another Swiss city, so he could be closer to Luther and Zwingli. All he had wanted was a quiet place to study, but he soon found himself with the task of helping a small group of Reformers. He took his job seriously and worked so hard for church reform that he made enemies who drove him out of Geneva. He lived for a few years in another town, Strasburg, where he taught some young students in his own apartment.

"But he continued to work on his plans, and after he returned to Geneva, he made a number of reforms in the church there. He changed the worship service, making it more simple. The significant parts were to be Bible reading and preaching. His followers wrote new kinds of church music, too, making hymns out of the Psalms in the Bible. One of them, called Old Hundredth because it is taken from Psalm 100, you may have heard in your own church:

All the people that on earth do dwell
Sing to the Lord with cheerful voice.
Him serve with mirth, his praise forth tell;
Come ye before him and rejoice.

Of course, all the people had to sing *the tune* . . . no one was allowed to sing harmony parts—or at least not in church.

"Calvin was particular about obedience in church. If people fell asleep because they had stayed up too late the night before, they were waked up by the ushers. People who didn't go to church were fined by the city government." Dr. Jackson paused. "Any comments?"

"Yes," said Jason. "Why did the *city* fine people for not going to church?"

"Ah, yes. Well, Calvin had reformed Geneva so thoroughly that anyone who wasn't part of the *Reformed* Church was forced to move out. He wanted Geneva to be a Christian city. And of course by Christian, he meant Protestant.

"Calvin was a great Christian thinker, like Augustine. And like Augustine, he wrote a number of big books. One of them is called *The Institutes of the Christian Religion,* in which he described the whole Christian faith. He began with God, because God made everything—the world and everything in it. God is very powerful and good, but ordinary people cannot understand God and all that he does. All we know is that whatever he does is right.

"Remember the story of Abraham in the Bible? Calvin liked that story because it told about Abraham's great faith in God. He was willing even to give up his own son, Isaac, if God said he must. Even if he could not understand, he still believed. Because Abraham had such great faith, God made his follow-

99

ers, the Jewish people, his *chosen* people. When Jesus came, God included Christians among his chosen people. And now, thought Calvin, the *Calvinists* had become God's chosen people. Of course, Catholics and Lutherans and others said he was wrong. There were many arguments about whether God's chosen people were the Calvinists, or all true Christians, no matter what their church—or maybe all people who love God, even if they aren't members of a church.

"Anyway, Geneva became famous. Many people came to see the wonderful Christian town. Others came because they were religious refugees . . . many were Protestants who had been driven out of France, which was largely Catholic. Geneva opened its gates to thousands of Protestant refugees.

"One of the most important foreign visitors to Geneva was John Knox, who came from Scotland. In those times Scotland was a separate country, not connected with England, and her queen was a French Catholic. John Knox was one of the early Protestant leaders. Catholics didn't want the Reformers to spread dissatisfaction among the Scots, so they captured Knox and sent him to the *galleys* as a slave. He helped row a big ocean-going ship. After he was released, he fled to Geneva, and when he returned to Scotland, he took with him Calvin's Reformed religion. This became the Presbyterian Church of Scotland."

Pam had been thinking. Now she asked, "Why did people keep having to run away from their own countries? Why couldn't they stay home and worship the way they wanted?"

Dr. Jackson, half-laughing, half-sad, said, "We keep circling back to this question. In those times almost everyone thought there could be only one kind of true religion and that all other kinds were wrong. Only the 'true' kind should be supported by the people and by the government, so no one was free to worship differently. Those who had other ideas were driven out or thrown into prison. It was only later that some Christians had a new idea—that God was willing for his people to worship in different ways in different churches. The main thing was to love God and all his people. We call this idea religious freedom. But there was no place for it in the stormy years of the Reformation."

After a silence, Kristi spoke up. "I bet Francis, our statue, wouldn't drive people away because they believed differently. He loved everyone, didn't he?"

Dr. Jackson replied, "Yes, Kristi. But Francis was not a great ruler in the church. He left big decisions to others. Some Protestants during the Reformation felt the same way. But most of the *leaders* were sure that there was only one true way to worship, and that was *their* way."

"There must have been a lot of fights," said Jeff, "when the Catholics, and the Lutherans, and the Zwinglians and the Calvinists, too, all mixed it up."

"They even had religious wars for awhile, Jeff. Zwingli went out to battle with the troops of Zurich. He was their chaplain, the minister who went with them to war. In a great battle, Zwingli himself was killed, along with many young men. Nobody won the war. But Switzerland was divided into separate Catholic and Protestant sections. Those religious wars did not really settle anything. In Germany, too, when they finally were tired of fighting, they decided to let the rulers of the different sections decide whether theirs would be Protestant or Catholic.

"Next time we meet, we will talk about how the Reformation went underground."

Pam commented, "Our bridge is getting pretty full of people right along here. How can we get them all on?"

"V-e-r-y carefully!" Dr. Jack laughed.

Chapter 15

THE HIDDEN REFORMATION

Dr. Jackson arrived at the park later than his young friends, and he was certainly behaving strangely, Jeff thought. He walked softly and kept looking behind him as though he were afraid he was being followed. "We must change our meeting place," he whispered. "Where is the most secret place in this whole park? A place where we could hide if we didn't want anybody to find us. Do you know any place like that?"

Kristi and Pam looked at each other, and Pam said, "Dr. Jack . . . uh . . . Kristi and I . . . we know a secret place along the brook down there. It's in that unmowed part of the park. The only paths are the ones that have been made exploring. We know a nice shady place beside the brook. We go there sometimes. It would make a good hiding place."

Kristi added, "Yes, but don't tell anyone about it, OK? It's just for us today. But why do you want a secret place, Dr. Jack? We usually meet right here on the grass, with Francis for company."

"I'll explain when we get there. Lead the way."

The whole group trooped after Pam and Kristi, and Dr. Jackson began to talk as they walked along a narrow brushy path. "The Reformation story has some hiding in it today. The people we are talking

103

about were forced to worship in secret. None of them could say openly what he or she really believed, because in most countries their beliefs were against the law. Roman Catholic, Lutheran, Calvinist, Anglican countries—*all* had laws against them. There were only a few places where they could live and worship freely and openly.

"Of course some rulers were more strict than others. And sometimes the police were lazy or careless or just too busy. But a secret worshiper always had to be careful . . . or else willing to become a martyr—to be put in prison or killed."

"Gee, Dr. Jack," said Jason. "Who were those people? What kind of reform had to be hidden like that?"

"Here we are," interrupted Pam and Kristi together. They had reached a little brook, not very deep, with round rocks all over the bottom. There was a small clearing beside it, open enough for grass to grow. And there were even a few big rocks to sit on.

"This is a good place. Thanks, girls, for sharing it with us. We will keep your secret. Let's pretend now that it is against the law to meet like this. We have to be quiet. The police would like to catch us and put us in prison. We haven't committed a crime or done anything wrong. All we want is to come here to worship.

"Try to get some *feeling* of the way it was in those times when the Radical Reformers met to worship in their hidden places. Jason, those are the people we will talk about today: the ones who wanted *more* reforms in the church. They wanted to make it like the church of the early Christians and the apostles. They were not satisfied with the reforms made by Luther and the others. So both the Catholics and the other Protestants were against these people. They felt they were like the early Christians in the Roman Empire, when Christianity was illegal. So they had to hide. It was the only way they could follow Jesus."

Pam said, "I think they were right. If you are a Christian, following Jesus is the most important thing, even if it is against the law."

"It took courage to be a Christian then. These Radical Reformers had a lot of courage. They were not all part of a single group, though. There were several different leaders. And no one name, even Radical Reformers, fits them all. Some we call Anabaptist, which means *rebaptizers*. They believed baptism was only for people old enough to decide for themselves that they wanted to be Christian. They would not baptize babies or small children. But other groups were different. The people of one group called themselves spiritual, and would not have any sacraments at all. They said baptism was meaningless. Still another group believed that it was all right to baptize children.

"There were other differences. Some thought that true Christians should not resist their persecutors— that they should all be like lambs and suffer. Others thought that resistance in the name of the Lord was necessary—that they should all be like lions and fight back. Many lambs and many lions ended up in prison or were killed. A famous book called *The Martyrs' Mirror* tells the stories of those brave people."

Anna asked, "How can you tell the groups apart? It gets complicated with so many different ones."

"It does indeed get complicated," Dr. Jackson agreed. "One group was called the church Anabaptist. They worshiped in churches, as other Christian groups did. Another group, the no-church Anabaptist, did not believe in organized churches or baptism.

The people of a third group were revolutionaries. They believed Jesus would come back to set up a Christian kingdom, and they intended to help by overthrowing evil governments.

"One man said that he knew when Jesus was coming. It would be in the year 1533. He said he would be imprisoned by the police, and Jesus would come and free all the prisoners. He was right about the first part, but he died in prison.

"Most of the Radical Reformers were peaceful people, though. In fact, most were *pacifists,* which means they believed that all wars are unChristian. They felt they should not fight, but turn the other cheek, as Jesus taught in the Sermon on the Mount. They should love their enemies, and *help* people instead of fighting with them. Some were even put in jail for *that.*

"They were persecuted mainly because they did not believe their rulers had a right to tell them what to believe and how to worship. They were willing to obey the rulers, except in matters of religion. And in that, they wanted to be left alone. They wanted the freedom to believe and to worship as they chose. And the way they *chose* to worship was as the early Christians did—as nearly as they could.

"But they got into all kinds of trouble. People did not understand their ways because they were different. Sometimes they even made trouble for themselves. Once one of them stood up in the middle of a Swiss Reformed Church service and cried out, 'Not you, but I, have been called to preach!' "

"Whew," said Anna, "I'll bet *that* didn't go over too well."

"Neither did some of their other activities," said Dr. Jack. "One group burned the New Testament. They quoted Jesus as saying, 'The letter kills,' and they insisted that *letter* meant the words in the Bible. They thought it was better to let God lead them directly, without the Bible.

"One day in Zwingli's town, Zurich, some of the Radical Reformers put on a show: One of them baptized another, who had been a priest. Then they all baptized one another. Zwingli believed this was mistreating the sacrament of baptism and wanted it stopped. But there was no strong king in Switzerland, and there were lots of hiding places in the mountains."

Jason said, "If we were really hiding here, we would have to take turns being guard, to look out for soldiers or spies." And Kristi took a quick look over her shoulder.

"Of course," Dr. Jackson went on, "not all the Anabaptists or Radical Reformers had to stay in hiding. One group in Holland organized the Mennonite Church, named for Menno Simons. Many of that group later sailed to America, where they could worship freely. They settled in Illinois, in Kansas, and in Canada. A group of Swiss Mennonites settled in Pennsylvania."

Jeff said, "We know some Amish people who live near our grandfather's farm in Ohio. They wear old-fashioned clothes and still drive horses and buggies . . . but they sure do have nice farms."

"The Amish are much like the Mennonites, Jeff, but they cling even more to old ways; they believe the old ways are best. They won't own cars or televisions. They are an industrious people; most of them are farmers. Both Mennonites, who are more willing to have modern things, and the Amish, who are not, believe that Christians should simply follow Jesus and be good disciples. They try to obey the Sermon on the Mount. That is a difficult thing to do in today's world, where life gets more complicated every day.

"There is one unusual group that is very interesting—the Hutterites, named for their leader, Jacob Hutter. They, too, come from the Radical Reformation. They have a special belief, which they found in the New Testament book of Acts. There it tells that the early Christians shared all their possessions and that everybody helped everybody else when they had need. The Hutterites live together in small farm communities, or *communes,* like one great big family. They eat their meals together; they have a school for their children; they plant crops and harvest together. A few Hutterite communities have lasted to our time, scattered here and there across the western United States."

Pam said, "I don't think I'd like to live in a big group like that. I'd be put in with all the other children, and not see my mom and dad."

"Well, it's not as bad as that, Pam. You would still see your parents and do some things with them, but it would be different from our way of life, yes."

Anna said, "People wouldn't have much freedom to do what they wanted, would they? Everybody would have to do what *the group* wanted."

"True," Dr. Jackson said. "Sometimes things did *not* work out well, and the Radical Reformers had arguments about whose way was best. Sometimes they divided into different groups, such as the Mennonites and the Amish. But other Christians have this kind of problem, too. It's somewhat like children sharing toys. If all the toys belong to all the children, nobody has anything to call his own. If each child has his own toys only for himself, he can't play with any other toys. The best way is somewhere in between—some things you can say are your very own, yet many things that all share. Hutterites had special problems because they tried to share so much." Dr. Jackson paused.

"Thanks, Pam and Kristi, for sharing your hiding place. It's been just right for today. Next time at my house, and we will do some more work on our bridge."

And with a glance back at the little brook and the quiet clearing, they all started home.

Chapter 16

REFORM IN MERRY ENGLAND

Dr. Jackson had the sketch of the bridge taped to the wall of his den. His young friends spent some time poring over the figures that Anna and the professor had drawn in.

"There's Martin Luther!" said Kristi. "I can tell because he is a bit plump."

"Those must be Calvin and Zwingli," added Jason.

"And that," said Anna firmly, "is Menno Simons."

"Today," Dr. Jackson began, "we will add some English men and women. Reformation happened in Merry Olde England in a different sort of way."

The young people found places on cushions and carpet and were ready to listen.

"Why do they always call it *Merry* England?" Pam wanted to know.

"Well," said Dr. Jackson, "in those days England was an exciting place to live. There were world explorers like Sir Walter Raleigh and Sir Francis Drake. There were fine writers like Edmund Spenser and William Shakespeare. And there were fine and brave religious leaders, too. The times of the Tudor family of rulers were exciting times indeed.

"One of the Tudor kings was Henry VIII, of whom I am sure you have heard."

"Yes," Jason said. "He was the one who had a lot of wives."

Dr. Jackson nodded. "Six. His first queen was Catherine of Aragon. The king wanted a male heir—a son who would rule after him. But only one of their six children survived, a sickly daughter named Mary. A woman could rule in England—but the times were dangerous, and Henry wanted a *prince*. Besides, he was quite taken with a lady of the court, Anne Boleyn. So Henry decided to divorce Catherine and marry Anne. There was trouble, though. The pope would not allow this divorce. He even said that he would excommunicate, or 'unchurch,' Henry. But King Henry VIII was not ready to be bossed around by the pope. 'Go ahead,' he said. 'I'll make my *own* church, and *I* will be the head of it myself.' And he did—he established the Church of England, the Anglican Church."

Pam asked, "But Dr. Jack, what about the son King Henry wanted? Did Queen Anne have a son?"

"Unfortunately, when Anne had a baby, it too was a girl. Henry was so disappointed he threw Anne into the Tower of London, a prison. There she was tried, convicted, and killed. The baby was named Elizabeth, and she became one of England's greatest rulers. But that was later. Elizabeth was raised with her half-sister, Mary. In time, they both became queens of England.

"Meanwhile, Henry looked around for another queen and found Jane Seymour. At last, this wife bore him a boy child. The people were so happy that they quite forgot about poor Queen Jane, who had died in childbirth. Henry named his son Edward. Later on, Henry married three other women—one at a time, of course."

"Did Edward grow up and become king?" Kristi asked.

"Yes, he did, when he was only nine years old. But let's look at what happened to the church in England after King Henry broke with the pope. First, the king became the head of the church in England. Second, he abolished the monasteries and took their property. Third, he ordered the revision of the worship service.

"The Archbishop of Canterbury, who was 'head bishop' in England, was a very wise man named Thomas Cranmer. He was given the task of writing the *liturgy*—the words of the worship service—for the new Anglican Church. Wisely, Cranmer kept many parts of the old form of worship. But he also made some changes. The result was part Catholic, part Protestant—a kind of compromise. From his work came the *Book of Common Prayer* used today by Anglicans and Episcopalians. Many parts of it are used by a number of other churches, also.

"At about that time, William Tyndale and some others translated the Bible into English. Tyndale was educated at Oxford and Cambridge universities. He thought old Wyclif had been right—that the Bible ought to be in the language of the people. And Tyndale had two tools that Wyclif had not had: knowledge of the biblical languages, Hebrew and Greek, and the printing press. He could print thousands of Bibles, instead of producing only a few handwritten ones.

"But his plan got him in trouble with the government. King Henry worried that people might get wrong ideas from the Bible (wrong from *his* point of view, that is). For instance, Jesus taught that God loves all people equally. What if people read that and commoners began to get the idea that they were as important as the noblemen? So Henry forbade any unofficial translations. Tyndale had to flee to Germany. There he set up his presses and printed the first English Bible. When the German government discovered what he was doing, he had to flee again. But he went right back to his project. He printed more Bibles and smuggled them secretly into England.

"Conservative Reformers like Thomas More disagreed with what Tyndale was doing. Finally he was caught, in what is today Belgium. He was cast into a horrible prison, convicted of heresy, and killed. People said that his last words were, 'Lord, open the king's eyes.' "

"But why did Mr. More and the king think the Bible was a *bad* book?" Pam asked. "Today we call it the Good Book."

"It wasn't that Henry and Sir Thomas believed the Bible was *bad,* but that it was *dangerous.* They thought it would be better if only priests had the Bible. Priests were trained to read it. Commoners might misunderstand it. It *is* a complicated book, you know."

Pam said, "But the best way would be to educate the people so they could all understand the Bible."

"True, Pam, but public education was something no one had even dreamed of then. Later on, King Henry did allow an English Bible to be printed and put into churches, although it was kept under the control of the ministers and used under their direction. But it surely wasn't Tyndale's Bible.

"At last Henry died, and young Edward became King Edward VI. How would it feel to be a nine-year-old king of England?"

"I'd be scared. I wouldn't know how to do it," Jason said.

"I think Edward felt the same way. But he had

already had some training. And besides, he had help. When a king or queen is too young, the government appoints a *regent,* or guardian, to do most of the work. Edward only signed his name on new laws and sat on the throne to receive visitors. I think you could do that quite well, Jason."

"Well, I guess so, but it still would be scary."

"Anyway, during the six years that Edward was king, the reform movement grew in England. The church became more Protestant. Unfortunately, the young king was not healthy, and when he was fifteen, he died. This meant that Mary, daughter of the first Queen, Catherine, became ruler of Anglican England.

"Now, Queen Mary was a Roman Catholic, so she promptly insisted that the English church come back to the pope and to Roman Catholicism. She threw the Reformers in jail, including Cranmer and two important bishops, Latimer and Ridley. They were tried for heresy, and all three were burned alive. This made them heroes and martyrs. Queen Mary had many people who disagreed with her religion put to death—close to three hundred, altogether.

"A man named John Foxe collected all the stories he could find about what Mary was doing and put them in a book, along with other martyr stories. Foxe's *Book of Martyrs* became as famous as *The Martyrs' Mirror.* This gave Queen Mary a very bad reputation."

"I should think so!" said Anna huffily.

"Was she the one they called Bloody Mary?" Jeff asked.

"Yes," Dr. Jackson said. "Then Mary died, and Elizabeth became queen. Her long reign was really the best time for Merry England. Under Good Queen Bess, as they sometimes called her, England became very strong. Elizabeth supported sailors and soldiers and explorers like Raleigh and Drake, and artists, and writers, and musicians, and architects.

"Queen Elizabeth changed England's religion back to the Anglican Church of her father, Henry, and helped establish it firmly between extreme Protestantism and the Catholic faith. It became a 'bridge' church, arching over the gulf between the opposite sides.

"One thing more about the English reform: Some people did not like this half-Protestant half-Catholic church. Roman Catholics wanted to stay with their old church headed by the pope, and some of them were punished by the government. Others wanted to make the whole chuch Reformed. The government punished some of *them,* too. But they kept on working for reform. They became the Puritans, and we will talk about them next time. But now it's time to draw the Tudor rulers of England on our bridge of church history. Here, Anna, is the sketching pencil. Next week we'll meet the Pilgrims."

"Hey," said Kristi. "Can we have a Thanksgiving dinner, then? The Pilgrims started Thanksgiving, didn't they?"

"Well, it might be hard to have a big turkey dinner right here in the park. But I have an idea! Everybody can bring something for an after-school snack. Bring enough of whatever you want for everyone. We'll share—like the Hutterites, and like the Pilgrims, too. But remember to tell your parents you aren't likely to want much for supper. That sound OK?"

"Terrific!" said Pam.

"Sure!" "Great!" agreed the others.

Chapter 17

THE PILGRIMS AND THEIR FRIENDS

Pam was the first to appear, carrying a sack of big shiny apples. Then came Dr. Jackson, with a thermos full of chocolate milk and a blanket. Kristi appeared with a box of graham crackers, and Jason and Jeff, with cookies. Last was Anna, out of breath.

"I was almost here," she gasped, "and I forgot . . . I mean I remembered I forgot . . . I mean . . ." All the young people laughed at Anna's mixed-up words.

Jason said, "Aha! You forgot your share of our treat."

"Well, I had to go back for it," said Anna. "Here it is." And she placed on the spread-out blanket a thermos of punch and a plastic bag of miniature candy bars.

"Well," said Dr. Jackson, "if we are going to have a Pilgrim Thanksgiving snack time, we should begin it with a blessing." And he did.

Then everyone shared the goodies. When their real hunger was attended to, and they had settled down to the last contented munching, Dr. Jackson began the story again. "We've had fun today, and it helps us think about the Pilgrims. They were one small group who sailed from England and settled in New England, in the part we now call Massachusetts. Many of them wanted a new life, away from the laws and customs of old England. They wanted freedom to worship the way they believed was right. The Pilgrims felt they couldn't do that in England.

"But there were many others, also called Puritans, who didn't come to the New World. *Puritan* is from the word *pure*. They wanted to make the Church of England pure. We can think of them as Reformers, like the ones we have learned about already, except that they lived about a hundred years later. There had already been an English Reformation, with the Anglican Church. But the Puritans took still another step in reform."

"Our bridge sure is getting full of Reformers," said Jason.

Jeff nodded. "Seems like they were needed, though," he said.

Dr. Jackson nodded, too. "The story of the Puritans is complicated. There were many leaders, but primarily of two kinds. First there were those who wanted to reform the Church of England—to stay in it and make it better, more Christian, more biblical. Then there were those who finally gave up trying to reform that church and separated from it. They started new churches. They believed that only by starting over could they make the church pure. They were called *Separatists* because they separated from the official church.

"At one big meeting, called the Hampton Court Conference, the Puritans came with a long list of changes they wanted made. The king granted only one of their requests, but it was a big one. King James I approved a new translation of the Bible into English. There were already other English Bibles, but they were not altogether correct, and sometimes the writing was not very good. The new translation, done by famous scholars, was a very good one. We still use it; we call it the King James Version of the Bible. Many people think it is the most beautiful translation we have.

"Today we also use other translations, more modern and more accurate, too, because the writers can refer to recently discoverd old documents. But when you hear your Sunday school teacher or minister use such words as *thee* and *thou,* you are listening to the old English of the King James Bible. Some of it is a little hard to understand today, because languages change. When the King James Bible quotes Jesus as saying 'Suffer the little children to come unto me,' it does not mean that he wanted little children to be hurt. The word *suffer* used to mean *allow* or *permit.* Modern versions usually translate that line '*Let* the children come to me.'

"But that is all the Puritans received in the way of reform. The king and the leaders of the Church of England were against the other changes. Church affairs were mixed up with political affairs, and finally there was a war between the Puritans and the government. One Puritan leader, Oliver Cromwell, became general of the Puritan army and won all the battles. He felt that God was on his side, and he thought that winning proved that.

"So for awhile, the Puritans ran the country. They made the changes they wanted and 'purified' the church. They discarded customs they thought came from the Roman Catholic Church. Catholics made the sign of the cross, so that was out; they had fancy robes for priests, so that was out; they used rings in weddings, had organs *in* and crosses *on* churches, so those were out. Pure Christians rejected all that. Pure Christians should live pure lives. And the Puritans were sure they knew what they must do to be pure. They must remember Sunday as the Lord's Day: always church service on Sunday; no work of any kind; no silly games. Puritan children learned about Sunday in their *Catechism* (little book of questions and answers):

> **Question:** How is the Sabbath to be sanctified?
> **Answer:** The Sabbath is to be sanctified by a holy resting of all that day, even from such worldly employments and recreations as are lawful on other days, and by spending the time in public and private exercises of God's worship, except so much as is to be taken up in works of necessity and mercy."

"But I can't understand all those big words," complained Pam. "Couldn't they say it easier?"

"Puritans believed in saying things plainly, Pam. But they did not make things very clear for children. Maybe next time we'll talk about being a child in those times. Want to?" Anna and Jeff nodded, remembering their discussion of children during the very early times. Being an American child in colonial times would have been difficult, too.

Dr. Jackson continued: "Back to the Puritans now. Some of them were not satisfied with getting rid of old customs. They wanted to do away with even more and start with a really pure church, with only 'true' Christians in it. A number of arguments developed and resulted in the separation of a number of people. Some became Presbyterians. Some became Congregationalists. Some became Baptists. Some became Quakers. Finally later, the English people and their government decided that different kinds of Christians in different churches could live together without fighting and persecuting one another. That was really the beginning of the idea of religious freedom. Before that, however, there was much trouble."

Dr. Jackson got up and walked around the picnic blanket to lean against a tree. "Let me tell you the story of one man," he said. "This man wrote a book that became famous. He called it *Pilgrim's Progress*. The man's name was John Bunyan, and he grew up in a little village named Elstow. He had some hard times himself. His mother died when he was fifteen. Later on his wife, Mary, died too. He had the task of raising their four children himself—and one of them was blind."

That would be pretty hard for one parent to do alone, thought Jeff.

"These sad experiences caused John Bunyan to do a lot of thinking about life and about religion. He read the Bible. He prayed. He changed his life and became a devoted Christian. Then, he said, he 'began to look into the Bible with new eyes, and read as I never read before.' He became a preacher. But at that time, preaching was still illegal unless the person was a minister of the official church, the Church of England. Bunyan was only a working man, not a trained minister at all. So he was arrested, tried, and put in jail.

"While he was in prison with not much else to do, he began to write. First he wrote just for his own pleasure. But by the time he had served his long jail sentence, he had written a whole book. It was the story of a man named Christian, who was on his way to heaven. And it was an exciting story. On his journey, Christian ran into many dangers, but he finally reached his goal, which was heaven. Bunyan did two things at the same time in *Pilgrim's Progress*. He told an exciting adventure story, and he also told how a Christian should live in the world.

"Bunyan, like all Christians of his time, spent a lot of time thinking about heaven and hell. Life was a time of trial, to decide where you would end up. Life had spiritual dangers and temptations. Bunyan named them in his book. There was a muddy mire in the road which he called the Slough of Despond. Then there were the Hill of Difficulty, the Valley of Humiliation, the Monster of Apollyon, Doubting Castle, and Giant Despair.

"But along this dangerous road were helpers: a Wicket Gate with a kindly gate keeper; the Wayside Cross; friends like Faithful and Hopeful and Great-heart and Mercy and Old Honest. At last Christian reached the Delectable Mountains which represented the church. At the end of his life, he crossed the big river and reached the gates of heaven. And the angels sang with joy."

Kristi broke in, "Why don't *we* know that story? I never heard of it . . . and it sounds exciting."

"Well, Kristi, some people do know that story today. But it is out of fashion, like old-fashioned clothes. It uses old-fashioned words and images, but it *is* a good story. Maybe you can find a copy of *Pilgrim's Progress* in the library. Some versions are shortened and a little easier for children to read."

"What happened to Bunyan?" Jason wanted to know. "You said he got out of jail."

"He became minister of a Baptist church in Bedford, England, and he had a good life. By that time, Bunyan and others like him could worship more freely, in their own churches."

"High time!" muttered Jeff.

"Well, yes," Dr. Jackson agreed. "The Quakers were another of the groups that grew out of the Puritan movement. George Fox, the leader of the Society of Friends (as the Quakers called themselves), was a very interesting man. He was something like the Radical Reformers, in that he wanted extreme reforms. He read the Bible, of course, like John Bunyan. But he decided that even the Bible was not enough. A Christian ought to be guided by the Spirit of God. Jesus had promised to be with his followers and guide them through the power of the Holy Spirit. Fox experienced this sort of guidance in his own life, and he called it the Inner Light. He felt that guidance of the Spirit of God within him helped him be more Christian. And he thought that the Bible and the Inner Light were enough. Churches and services of worship were not really necessary. So he and his followers met in ordinary houses. They did not have preachers or sermons or services or sacraments. They had 'silent meetings' and listened for the Spirit, or Inner Light. Theirs was, and still is, genuine worship, you know. It's just different from that of other groups."

"Did he get into trouble for being different?" Jason asked. "Seems like everybody always did, in those days."

"And in these days, too, sometimes," Jeff added.

"Well," Dr. Jackson went on, "George Fox was a brave man. But he was also a bit brash—maybe a bit abrasive, if you know what I mean."

"Like . . . *scratchy?*" asked Anna.

"Yes. That's it. Some people called him a troublemaker. For example, he would not take his hat off—inside or out. Not even in the presence of the king. And that seems unnecessarily . . . *scratchy.* Sometimes he would visit other churches and interrupt the services by talking louder than the minister."

Jeff was puzzled. "But I thought the Quakers are pacifists . . . that they don't believe in war or fighting."

"You are right, Jeff. The Society of Friends is one of the peace churches. But George Fox himself had a quick temper. He did not believe in war, but he could cause a lot of excitement—and he did. He spent a good bit of time in and out of jail. The later Quakers were, and are, a peaceful people."

Jeff nodded. That sounded more like what he knew of the Quaker church. He added, "It's kind of interesting, though, that not all the founders of the faith were *perfect* people. I think it's neat that one old Quaker was not only brave and devout, but also stubborn and scratchy!" Jeff half-smiled as he stopped, and he turned a little red. That was probably the most he had said since their group had first started meeting.

Dr. Jackson smiled, too. "Right, Jeff. It makes *our* humanness seem more acceptable, doesn't it? Well, there is more to the Christian story. But next time, let's take another look at the lives of children. We have talked about children of the early Middle Ages. Now we are leaving the long medieval arch of our bridge and entering the modern era. What was it like to be a child about three hundred years ago? That's for next time."

Chapter 18

RECESS: BEING A CHILD
IN EARLY MODERN TIMES

Kristi was last to arrive at the park. She greeted the group, turned her skateboard over on the grass to provide herself with a seat, and wedged herself firmly between the wheels. Dr. Jackson laughed, and then began to talk.

"Remember," he said, "how we learned about the hard life of many children in olden times? Way back on the first arch? Remember, too, that in spite of hard times, children managed to be happy and grow up? Parents were not very good at caring for their families; nevertheless, most of them loved their children. At that time, the approved child-rearing policies were to either ignore children, or make them work to serve adults. Of course, almost everybody then had to work hard just to live and keep going. Sometimes children were abused. (Sometimes they still are). Sometimes they were sold or given away to be servants to other people.

"Big changes came some time after the Reformers. Remember that Martin Luther said that a Christian family was the closest of all to heaven? That he loved his own children dearly? That marriage and family life were better than unmarried single life? All this helped make family life better.

"Long before the Reformation, the church had

taught that it was wrong to abandon children, or give them away, or sell them. Laws were made against those things. But it was only in modern times that people began to learn a little more about children— about what they are really like. People had really thought that a child was just a miniature adult.

"We can tell that by the way children were dressed. Something else you could tell by the people's clothing was their place in society: whether they were peasants, noblemen, shoemakers, whatever. Rich people wore fancy clothes; poor people, plain ones. But children were still dressed in what seem to us funny ways. Until they were about five years old, both boys and girls were dressed in long robes or dresses. If they were rich, the clothing was decorated with lace and ribbons. Under the dresses there were two or more underskirts."

"You couldn't do much running and playing and climbing trees dressed like that," Pam remarked.

"Boys wore the dresses and underskirts, too, but sometimes the outside robe was open in front, instead of closed like the girls'. At about the age of seven, little boys had an exciting time. They got to wear their first pair of pants, just like their fathers'—knee breeches, in well-to-do families. At that age, boys began to dress differently from girls. But they were dressed like grown men, in every detail. And girls were dressed like miniature women. There were no clothes at all for just children.

"That was the custom from about Luther's time until Revolutionary times in America. Finally people began to realize that children needed a different sort of clothing. Children are more active than adults. They need more freedom of movement. People began to make children's clothes a little lighter, a little simpler.

"Changes in clothing and customs slowed while Victoria was queen of England. She was very conservative, perhaps a little stuffy, and did not like many modern ideas. Most little girls still wore long dresses and numerous petticoats. And many little boys wore little velvet suits. Sometimes little girls in the country had the freedom to run and jump, but when they were about sixteen, they had to begin to dress like 'ladies,' in ankle-length dresses, tight collars, and corsets.

"People also were very conservative about discipline. In the Old Testament, they found the line about spare the rod and spoil the child. So they *used* the rod freely. Victorians thought children should be seen and not heard. That meant they were to stay out of the way. Almost all children knew how it felt to be spanked. Sometimes there were really hard whippings.

"And it was the same in school. Children were spanked soundly, usually right in front of the class. Or their knuckles were whacked with a ruler. The idea was to teach discipline, obedience, and good behavior. They thought that was the only way children would learn.

"One reason for all this strict discipline was the Puritans' belief about life. All Christians believed that people could not be good all by themselves. They all needed God's help, even little babies. This was why some people baptized their babies. They reasoned that if all people are naturally bad without God, then children must be especially bad. 'Children are naturally selfish and obstinate and careless and lazy,' said the Puritans. 'That is why they must be punished—to show them the right way. Then they will learn how to be generous and kind and careful and industrious.'

"There was a little book for children that was used

in Puritan times, called *The New England Primer*. Children could learn the alphabet with verses that also taught religious lessons. The first one said,

> In Adam's fall
> We sinned all.

The second one read,

> Thy life to mend
> This *Book* attend.

Another said,

> The idle *Fool*
> Is whipt at school.

Another poem in the little book went this way:

> Fear God all day,
> Parents obey,
> No false thing say,
> By no sin stray,
> Love Christ alway,
> In secret pray,
> Mind little play,
> Make no delay
> In doing good.

The Puritans thought so much about God as judge that they sometimes forgot about God as love."

Kristi commented, "I don't think children had much fun back then. They all had to work so hard, and people treated them mean and wouldn't let them play."

Pam responded, "But Kristi, work is not bad if it really helps. Children had important chores to do.

They were busy with real jobs, right along with everybody else in the family. They were *needed*. In that way, they were *some*body. Today lots of children are treated like *nobodies*."

Jason said, "I guess it wasn't so bad. At least Christian parents loved their children and helped them grow up right. Besides, boys could go fishing and hunting for food with their fathers. That part would be good, even if it was part of the work."

Dr. Jackson said, "Slowly the old ideas changed. Some Christian parents had always been more liberal. Important writers like Jean Jacques Rousseau and others believed that children should be raised and taught by good example, rather than by harsh discipline. A child should be encouraged to *be* and *grow* like a child. That way, he or she would learn more and become a better person. Dress should be sensible and practical. Discipline should be gentle and helpful. Loving concern could work wonders. It's strange that more Christians did not learn this sooner. It is right there in the New Testament in the teachings of Jesus.

"One person who really understood children was Charles Kingsley, who wrote some famous books. He knew that children were people in their own right. And then there was Lewis Carroll. Most of you know him as the author of that wonderful story, *Alice in Wonderland*. Almost *no*body wrote books for children then. But he knew that children have vivid imaginations and that they love stories."

"I know that book," said Kristi. "Alice went through a magic looking glass and found a different world, with bad queens and nice people and everything—even a funny cat that had a smile that stayed there even when the cat was gone."

"Right. Maybe *we* should be grinning like Cheshire

cats because we are living in modern times. You have more freedom than children in the past. There were other important changes, too. Parents began to learn how important it is to be with and play with their children. Children used to have nursemaids to look after them. Now mothers and fathers like to be with their children and do things together when they can. In some families that means being with grandparents and aunts and uncles, too. And in some families it means a single parent, working to make a good life. *No* family is perfect. People have problems today, just as they have always had. But most young people are better off today than they were in those days."

"Yeah," said Kristi. "Just think, we're the first generation in the whole world to have skateboards!" And with a laugh, she was up and off on hers—the wheels takata-clicking on the sidewalk cracks.

Chapter 19

JOHN WESLEY AND
THE METHODIST REVIVAL

The "littler ones," as Jeff sometimes thought of them, walked up the steps of the university chemistry building as though they came there every day. But he walked up more slowly. Maybe he felt a little shy because it *was* a university . . . and he was still a middle schooler. Or maybe he was somewhat in awe of the sciences. He followed the others up the steps and was relieved to see Dr. Jackson open the door for them. Good, Jeff thought. At least we won't get lost inside.

Dr. Jackson greeted the boys and girls cheerfully and led them down the hall to a chemistry laboratory.

"This is not much like our usual meeting place," he began. "But I had a special reason for wanting us to come *here* to talk today. My friend in the chemistry department said we could meet in his lab, so here we are."

Jeff looked around at the equipment, wishing he knew what it was all used for. He could identify the Bunsen burners, and of course, test tubes . . . he wondered at the different shaped flasks and beakers and coiled tubing. Dr. Jackson was saying, "Maybe this will give us a feel for the times. Three hundred years ago, young people didn't *have* science classes."

"Goody," said Kristi. "I hate science."

"Well, maybe you'll change your ideas later on, Kristi. Working in a room like this might be pretty exciting." Jeff nodded his head in agreement.

Dr. Jackson went on, "But our main reason for meeting here today is that we are going to talk about John Wesley and the revival of the church. Wesley lived at a time when educated people were beginning to think more about science. They were really just beginning to use scientific methods. What do we mean by that, Jeff?"

"It means thinking about a problem and then trying out answers to see if they work—doing experiments."

"That's a good definition. Scientists have found that many things in life can be explained by gathering enough facts. Not everything, of course, but many things can be studied and measured. In Wesley's time, science was just beginning to become important. People were just beginning to think in terms of experimental discovery.

"Now, some people became very excited about these new ideas. They thought *everything* could be explained by science. Religion, they said, is un-scientific. So it must be just superstition, or perhaps just magic tricks. Religion is not true, they said. Only science is true. It believes in only what can be measured. And religious faith can't be measured. God can't be measured. Therefore religion is not real.

"Only a few people went that far with their reasoning. But quite a few others said that religion was all right as long as it agreed with science. These people were called deists. They believed in God, but only when God fit in with the ideas of the scientists.

"Then many people developed bad habits. Some drank too much liquor, while others wasted their money in gambling or spent all their time at shows

133

and games. And since many of them no longer believed in God, they didn't go to church anymore. Also at that time, many people were out of work because of the economic conditions. So there were many poor people in England when John Wesley and his brother Charles were growing up in Epworth.

"John Wesley did not disagree with the new ideas of science. In fact, he was very interested in many experiments. He was a well-educated young man and knew how to use his mind. But John saw the sad results when scientific thinking was used on non-scientific problems. He saw, too, the sad results of too much drinking and careless pleasure. And he felt sorry for the poor. He became a leader of what we call the Evangelical Revival. He and his friends wanted to wake up the church to the dangers of the times. The revival was called evangelical because it placed most importance upon the *good news* of the Christian gospel which we find in the New Testament. Wesley was the greatest hero of the revival in England. And he was the founder, though that was not his intention, of the Methodist Church."

"I know about John Wesley," said Anna. "I have a book about him. It tells about how he grew up in a great big family with lots of brothers and sisters."

"That's a good place to begin, Anna. Can you tell us anything about his boyhood?"

"I know his father was a minister in the English church. And he had a wonderful mother. Her name was Susanna. I know John had an older brother, Samuel, and you already talked about Charles. But mostly, John had sisters. Let's see, there was Emilia, the oldest, and then Susanna and Molly and Hetty and Nancy, and—oh yes, younger than John were Patty and Kezzy, the littlest."

"Splendid," said Dr. Jackson. "*I* certainly couldn't

have named all the sisters. Yes, John's mother Susanna was a remarkable woman. She took care of all her children and began their education early. She was very systematic. Some people today might think she was *too* systematic. But in that large family, her ideas worked.

"On his or her fifth birthday, each child learned the alphabet—all of it, that day. The next day, she began to teach the child to read little verses in the Bible. With their mother's help, they each read all the way through the Bible. When they were finished, they all knew how to read, and they also knew a lot about the Bible. And that, of course, was exactly what Susanna wanted. John Wesley never forgot the strong influence of his mother. Later, when he was grown, he was able to talk with her about religious beliefs and problems."

Anna added, "The children had to behave. Nobody got away with anything. They were spanked when they were naughty, or even noisy."

"Maybe that's why John was such a strong leader, Anna," Dr. Jackson said, teasingly.

"But before we leave John's Epworth home, let me tell you the story of the big fire. One night the family was awakened by the smell of smoke and cries of 'Fire! Fire!' The nursemaid gathered the children and hurried them out to safety. She called John, who was six years old, but he was too sleepy, became confused, and didn't follow her. The *rectory,* as the minister's house was called, began to blaze up fiercely—and suddenly Susanna realized that John was still inside. She tried to go back for him, but people stopped her. Then someone saw John at a second-story window. By now the roof was beginning to burn. So one young man climbed up on the shoulders of another man and could just reach the little boy—and pulled him out of the roaring fire. When they thought about it later, both he and his mother were sure that God had helped rescue John because there was some great work he wanted him to do. John was, they said, 'a brand plucked from the burning.'

"When John was a teenager—a little older than you, Jeff, he was sent off to a school called Charterhouse. These days, you would think it was terribly strict. But he received a good education there and went on to Oxford University. At Oxford he became more serious about the Christian faith. He became a leader of a club that had been started by his brother Charles. It was called the Holy Club. The student members studied the Bible together, shared prayer, and helped people in need—the poor and those in jail. Other students at Oxford joked about these serious young men. They called them Bible Moths. Then someone started calling them Methodists, because they were so methodical about their religious life. And the name stuck.

"When John graduated, he came to America to be chaplain of the new little colony of Georgia. He wanted to preach to the wild Indians. But he couldn't find any Indians to preach to, since most of them had gone farther into the forest to get away from the settlers.

"In Georgia, John fell in love with a young girl named Sophie Hopkey. But he was not ready to marry. He thought he should remain unmarried, like a Catholic priest, to do his work.

"Wesley was unhappy in Georgia. He had arguments with many people. He thought he was a failure, and after two years, he sailed back to England. It was in the middle of winter and very gloomy. Wesley felt gloomy inside, too. He thought he was not a good minister, or even a very good Christian. This made him very sad.

"But back home, with the help of his friends and his brother Charles, he recovered his faith and found that it was stronger. One night in the spring, he went to a religious meeting in London, on Aldersgate Street. There, as he said, 'I felt my heart strangely warmed.' He was sure that God was helping him in his search, helping him grow in faith."

Jason broke in. "Was Wesley converted there? People talk about being converted."

"Some say so. But really Wesley had been 'converted' long before. He was already a Christian. The experience at Aldersgate only made his faith stronger and clearer. Most people become Christians in stages, or steps, not all at once. Aldersgate was an important step, but not the only one—not the first one, and not the last. Perhaps we could say that it was one of many conversion experiences.

"For the rest of his life, John Wesley was leader of the Wesleyan movement in England. He did not want it to be a separate church. He wanted to keep it within the Church of England. He organized what he called *societies* for group worship and study. People who wanted to grow in faith came to the societies, or they became part of even smaller groups called *class meetings*. As an aid to the worship of 'the people called Methodist,' Charles Wesley wrote many fine hymns. Many of them are still sung by United Methodists, and by people of other churches, too. One of them begins:

> O for a thousand tongues to sing
> My great Redeemer's praise,
> The glories of my God and King,
> The triumphs of his grace!

137

Actually, Charles Wesley wrote more than seven thousand hymns.

"Some people in the Anglican Church did not like the new ways of the Methodists. They said all sorts of bad things about Wesley and tried to make him stop his work. Most of the bishops opposed what he was doing. When one told him he had no right to preach in another pastor's parish, Wesley replied, 'I regard the whole world as my parish.'

"People who disagreed with Wesley would try to 'outshout' his sermon, or would interrupt him, once even by running an old cow into the crowd. More than once, angry mobs threatened him. But Wesley was a brave man. He would call to the mob leaders and challenge them to listen—to see if he said anything that wasn't true. Then he would preach a lively sermon. And again and again, some of those who had come to fight stayed to listen, and many became Methodists themselves.

"John Wesley traveled back and forth across England, and also into Scotland and Ireland and Wales. He often preached four or five sermons in one day—in a field, in front of a house, sometimes in a church. And he rode many miles a year on horseback.

"So Wesley preached on, and the Methodist movement grew. It did much to revive religion in England and helped the Anglican Church a great deal. The Evangelical Revival was a reformation like that of Luther, three hundred years before. In fact, Germany had a revival about the same time as Wesley's. It was called Pietism, and another movement in America was called the Great Awakening.

"After John and Charles Wesley died, the Methodists separated from the Church of England and organized the Methodist Church. In the United

States, this was called the Methodist Episcopal Church. In 1939, the Methodist Protestant Church and the two branches of the Methodist Episcopal Church joined to form The Methodist Church. Then in April 1968, The Methodist Church combined with the Evangelical United Brethren Church, which had a similar background and belief, and became The United Methodist Church.

"Well, why don't we leave a note of thanks on the blackboard for my friend who let us use his chemistry lab? Maybe our meeting here will help us remember the time—and the *mood* of the world—in which the Wesleys grew up."

Dr. Jackson wrote a note, and Anna drew a bridge under it, with John and Charles Wesley walking across it, singing!

Chapter 20

LAND OF THE PILGRIMS' PRIDE

"I have a question for you," Dr. Jackson began. "What is different about the story of Christianity in the United States—different from Europe and the Middle East, where it all began?"

"We have bigger churches," Kristi suggested.

"No," said Anna, "that can't be it. We've got some big churches all right. But they aren': as big as the old cathedrals in Europe."

Jeff spoke up. "I think we have more different kinds of churches. In most countries there is only one church, or only a few. We have all kinds."

"Why did that happen? Jeff is right. There are dozens of large denominations in the United States, and more than a thousand small ones. What made religion in this country different?"

Pam suggested, "Well, there are more different kinds of people here. They came from different places, and they brought their own churches with them."

"Good, Pam. What else?"

Kristi said, "Yes, and they had different languages, like Mr. and Mrs. Schneider next door to us. They speak German. Oh yes, and like Pam here. Some black people like to have churches of their own. Others like to worship in more mixed churches."

141

"You people certainly are sharp this afternoon," Dr. Jackson said. "Those are good reasons. In fact, you have brought up all the main ones. Jeff is right about more different kinds of churches in America. By contrast, in France people *are* French, and they are either Roman Catholic or Reformed . . . or they belong to no church at all. In Germany, people are Roman Catholics, or Lutherans, or Reformed, with a very few that belong to other groups. In England, there are more varieties, such as the Puritan churches and the Methodists. But the *main* church is the Anglican Church, the official Church of England."

"There are Quakers, too," added Anna.

"Yes. And all these churches, from all those countries, were brought to America. That is important, because no one church could claim that it was *the* one real true church in this country. No single one could become the *official* church. The others would want equal rights. So we ended up with freedom of religion. That means that each person, each family, can decide which church is best for it. The laws allow people to choose their own church— or no church at all. Many other countries have this freedom now. But the idea became important early here. It became the main idea in America."

"That means, though," said Jeff, "that sometimes people get into funny churches with funny ideas."

"Right, Jeff. That's what freedom is all about— freedom to be different. *You* may think the others are funny, but *they* don't."

Kristi said, "Dr. Jack, a girl in my class goes to a church that thinks it is right and everybody else is wrong and that only members of that church can ever go to heaven."

"Some groups do believe that their church is the

142

only true church and that all the others are wrong. And they have a right to believe that. But they do not have the right to bother the other churches. We call this tolerance. Tolerance is a part of freedom."

Kristi suggested, "If I am free, then I have to let you be free, too. Is that it?"

"That's what makes freedom of religion so important, Kristi. We have already said that many different people came from other places with different languages and customs and religious beliefs. But can you think of any churches that *began* in the United States?"

For a bit they were silent, trying to think. Finally Jason said, "Well, maybe the Christian Scientists? I think they started here. Adam, my friend, is a Christian Scientist. He says a woman in New England started their church."

"That's a good example, Jason. Mary Baker Eddy was founder of the Christian Science Church, and it *did* start in America. How about the Church of Jesus Christ of Latter-day Saints? They are sometimes called Mormons. That church began in New York state more than a hundred years ago."

"Yes," chimed in Jeff. "They are mostly in Utah now."

"Do you know how they got so far out west?" Dr. Jackson asked. Jeff shook his head, and the professor explained. "They had to leave their homes to find freedom to worship in their own ways. The Mormons were not treated well at first, even in what we think of as a country that has *always* granted religious freedom. So they migrated westward. Some of them stopped off in Missouri. The others went on to Utah. Can you think of any other groups that began in this country?"

Pam hesitated, then said, "Maybe some of the

black churches, like the National Baptists and the African Methodists?"

"Right, Pam. All Baptist and Methodist movements go back to English roots. But these black groups, or *denominations*, were organized in the United States. Why do some churches have all, or almost all, black members?"

Pam was ready on this one. "Because the black people of this country were treated badly. Long ago Negroes were brought to this country from Africa to be slaves and work on *plantations*. Those were big farms that raised cotton down South. But even free Negroes were not treated right. White people made them sit in separate places, even in the churches. So the black people left and started their own churches."

"I don't blame them," commented Kristi. "The church should have been *one* place where things like that didn't happen."

"Should have been," agreed Dr. Jackson, "but wasn't. And of course the problem of slavery involved *all* the churches. Some denominations, the Methodists and Presbyterians and Baptists, even divided over this question. The black churches were right in the middle of the struggle over slavery and the fight for freedom.

"One Christian who worked very hard to help the slaves was Harriet Ross Tubman. She was a courageous and resourceful black woman who belonged to the African Methodist Episcopal Zion (A.M.E.Z.) church. She herself was born a slave in Maryland. When she was only five years old, she already had serving work to do. At eleven or twelve, she was sent out to the fields to work. She married a free Negro, John Tubman, and before the Civil War she ran away and escaped to Pennsylvania.

"But that was just the beginning of her story. She

organized the underground railroad. It wasn't really a *railroad*, but a secret route which slaves followed from the South to the North, to escape to freedom. Along the route were *way stations*, friendly people who would hide the runaways in their houses or barns until they could rest a bit to continue on the next lap of the escape journey. Some fled to northern states, some all the way to Canada. The A.M.E.Z. church did much to keep the underground railroad going. Many of their local churches were hiding places. Harriet Tubman herself went back and forth all the time. Her home in Auburn, New York, was a way station. She also cared for escaped slaves in the A.M.E.Z. church in Rochester. She even went back down South to show slaves the way. That was a very dangerous thing to do, since she herself was an escaped slave."

"Ummm," said Anna. "She must have been a brave woman. I had heard about Harriet Tubman. But I never knew that about the *church*."

Dr. Jackson went on. "In the United States, Christianity grew differently from anywhere else in the world. Many kinds of churches came: Some were centuries-old organizations, like the Eastern Orthodox and the Roman Catholic, and even the Lutheran and Waldensian; others, like the Methodists and Moravians and Unitarians and Disciples were not so old. The important thing to remember is that all of them were—and are—Christian churches. All believe in Jesus as the founder of the Church. He did not start just one denomination—he founded the Universal Church—with a capital C. All together, we make up that one Church that Jesus founded in the beginning. Some groups, of course, still claim to be the only true church. But they all believe they have their roots and beginnings in the life and teachings of

Jesus. And most will agree that God gave his truth in different ways to different people. It is still God's truth. The churches in America agree that all churches should have equal rights."

"Here, now"—Dr. Jackson interrupted himself. "Let's stretch a bit. Everybody run once around the statue of Saint Francis for every famous American Christian you can think of ". . . and they were off and running.

"Hey, wait!" yelled Jason, after a few turns around the statue. "It's good to get up and stretch my legs, but I've lost track of any names."

"Yes," laughed the others, and collapsed again in a circle on the grass. When they had caught their breath, Dr. Jackson began once again with a question: "Do you know who was one of the greatest Christians in America?"

They looked at one another blankly.

"Billy Graham?" suggested Jason.

"Graham is well known today because he is on television a good bit," Dr. Jackson replied. "But he isn't the famous leader I'm thinking of. I'll tell you. Abraham Lincoln!"

Kristi said, "But he wasn't a Christian. He was a President!"

"Can't a President be a Christian, Kristi? True, Lincoln was not a *church member*. But he was raised a Christian. He knew the Bible very well. More important, he spent much time thinking about God's will. He thought of the United States as being a part of God's plan. That is why he fought against slavery and injustice the best way he knew. Some of his speeches are almost like sermons. One of the best is the very short Gettysburg Address. Some of you know parts of it. And another is the speech he made at his second inauguration.

"You see, some of the Christian faith has become part of the very life of this nation. Because we started as a Christian nation, because our roots are deep in faith, we have passed on to later generations some very Christian principles. The *Christian* heritage has become a part of the *national* heritage."

"Well, then" said Pam firmly, "another great American Christian was Martin Luther King. He was a great leader. And he was a minister, too."

"Right, Pam. You might say King began where Lincoln left off. Lincoln got rid of slavery. King fought race prejudice and injustice. Both believed in what they were doing, because they were Christians."

"And don't forget," Dr. Jackson added, "that some of the American leaders have been women. Like Mother Francesca Cabrini in the Roman Catholic Church. She spent her life helping people in need. And there have been many fine Protestant women—Frances Willard and Amanda Smith and Lucretia Mott and Cynthia Wedel. More and more churches now have women ministers, who bring their strengths and talent—and faith!—to the service of the Church."

Dr. Jackson reached out to put his hands on the shoulders of Pam and Kristi, who happened to be on either side of him. "Enough for today," he said. "The story of the Church in the United States *is* complicated, because there are so many different kinds of us! More next time!"

Chapter 21

FROM SEA TO SHINING SEA

The group settled down for the next segment of the story . . . and once again Dr. Jackson began with a question. "Remember, Kristi, that you said last time that Abraham Lincoln was not a Christian, just a President?" Kristi nodded, a little flustered. "Well, what churches *did* the Presidents belong to? Do you know any of them?"

They shook their heads. "I didn't know many, either," Dr. Jackson went on. "So I looked up a few. There is quite a variety. George Washington was Episcopalian. Rutherford Hayes was a Methodist. Woodrow Wilson was Presbyterian. Herbert Hoover was a Quaker. Harry Truman was a Baptist and so was Jimmy Carter."

"And John F. Kennedy was Catholic," added Jeff. "He was the first Catholic President."

"Right. This is one example of the way the Christian religion is woven all through American life.

"And here is another. We can see how religion has left its mark on different parts of the country. Look at the Southwest: Southern California, Arizona, and New Mexico. There you see strong Roman Catholic influence, because most of the early settlers were Spanish. What's the capital of New Mexico?"

"Santa Fe," answered Jason.

"Santa Fe means *Holy Faith,* in Spanish. The original name was Royal City of the Holy Faith of Saint Francis of Assisi. And there is San Francisco, in California—St. Francis, again, our friend here." Dr. Jackson reached out and patted the foot of Francis' statue. "Franciscans, led by Father Junipero Serra, founded missions all over the Southwest. Some of them became very famous."

"I know;" said Anna. "One is the mission that the swallows come back to every year."

"San Juan Capistrano," said Jeff.

"It was the same way in New England," Dr. Jackson went on. "Where the Pilgrims and the Puritans settled, they brought both their English customs and their faith. There are Congregational churches on the town greens. Roger Williams and the Baptists chose a Christian name for their city— Providence. The Quakers in Pennsylvania did, too— Philadelphia, City of Brotherly Love. You can find Christian marks like these all over the United States."

"Bethlehem, Pennsylvania, is one," said Jason.

"Sure. Next time your family takes a trip, watch for Christian names. . . . Next question: What do we mean by the Westward Movement?"

Jason chimed in. "That means the pioneers, going West. Through the wilderness forest, across the mountains, covered wagons, Indians, settlers, cowboys . . . things like that."

"Fine, Jason. Thousands of people moved West— along the rivers on flatboats, or overland on horses and in covered wagons. Some walked the whole way. They took what they could with them. And they took their Christian faith. Some churches were more interested than others in going along with the pioneers. Baptists and Methodists were especially good at it. Baptists had their farmer preachers, who could earn a living by farming and could preach, too. Methodists had their circuit riders. Those were preachers who rode horseback from place to place, starting little Methodist groups. They carried Bibles and hymn books in their saddle bags and came back again and again to each settlement. After awhile, these preachers built log chapels and started churches everywhere in this way. There were Disciples and Cumberland Presbyterians on the frontier, too. All these groups became very important to American life. They greatly influenced the West.

"And the West influenced the churches, too. Can you think how that might have happened? What would a frontier church be like? At first, it would be a clearing in the wilderness, with maybe a few log cabins around. They couldn't have a *big* church. There was no organ. No stained-glass windows. No cushioned pews. Worship would have to be very simple. The people, and many of the preachers, too, had very little education. Life was hard. The grave-yard beside the church would have quite a few graves in it—many of them children's graves.

"It was in this kind of situation that *revival meetings* began. They were popular on the frontier. A strong preacher would call a revival meeting, and people would gather from miles around. They would bring tents, or they would sleep in their covered wagons. The meetings would last for days. There was lots of preaching and singing. Hymn books were scarce, so the song leader would 'line out' the hymns—he would sing a line, and then the people would sing it back to him. They loved to sing the old gospel songs that they could learn easily. Preachers shouted and acted out their sermons. They told people how bad their sins were. They told them to

150

repent, to be sorry, and mend their ways. Many people were converted at revivals. They gave up their old ways of life and became good Christians."

Kristi wanted to know, "Did children get to go to the meetings?"

"Everybody came, even the babies. The meetings that were so big they were held outside were called *camp meetings.* The children loved to go to the camp meetings. It was something like going to summer camp . . . with the tents and the covered wagons. They had big picnics and lots of social time. At night they had big campfires. But most of all, they had preaching, all day long. All this was really quite a bit different from the traditional services of worship in the churches of the Old World, back in Europe. It was a new and distinctly American brand of Christianity."

"Sounds like fun," said Pam. "Wish I'd been there."

Dr. Jackson went on. "Now think abut this one. What else has been special about the Church in America? Besides having many different kinds, besides being separate from the government, and besides revivals and camp meetings?"

Anna had an idea. "Well, the churches were always doing something, not just sitting there. I mean, they were busy helping poor people, and orphans, and sick people, and old people. And they were busy spreading Bibles and things around."

"Good, Anna. The American churches have been full of action. Their Christian gospel has been a *social gospel,* which means an emphasis on doing things such as those you mentioned. We have already talked about one of their earliest and largest actions, the campaign against slavery. The churches were in the middle of that. Groups divided over

151

it, sometimes to avoid having to face the issue. But others faced it and tried to struggle through for *Christian* solutions to difficult problems. Some leaders, like Gilbert Haven in the Methodist Episcopal Church and Harriet Tubman in her A.M.E.Z. church, were very active in helping escaping slaves. Later on, the social gospel worked in other ways for justice, for fairness for everybody.

"There was man in New York whose name was Walter Rauschenbusch. His name is easier if you break it up into smaller pieces. Begin with a lion's roar—ROWWW! Then the part of your leg that hurts so much when you bang it—shin. Then a bush—ROWW-shin-bush. He became a teacher in a Baptist school for ministers. As a *little* boy, he had lived in Germany. Then his family came to America, and he had grown up in a poor section of New York City. He said about his boyhood, 'I had my kinks even then, and later on they became twists, loops, and knots.'

"Walter wanted to go to some foreign land to be a missionary. But as it turned out, he found his mission right in New York City. He knew the poverty on the West Side, which was a tough slum area. Children played in the streets because there was nowhere else to play—no parks, no playgrounds, no yards. Some people called that part of New York, Hell's Kitchen.

"Well, Walter Rauschenbusch became the minister of a church in Hell's Kitchen. He saw how poor, sick, lonely people suffered there. He kept his eyes and his heart open—and he discovered that the church could do a lot of things besides conduct worship services on Sundays. One thing he did was to provide some sandpiles for the slum children. That didn't cost much, and the children liked the sandpiles. He made friends with the children, and they began to come to Sunday school.

"Do you know the Bible verses in which Paul wrote about love? Walter said that love belongs in the slums . . . it is doing such things as giving little children sandpiles. Later on, this same Walter Rauschenbusch wrote important books about the social gospel. He described how Christian love fits into places where people have hard times, where people hurt. He believed that was an important way to follow Jesus."

"Sure makes sense to me," said Jason.

"Some people thought the social gospel went too far, though. They said the churches were teaching too much about social justice and not enough about repentance and forgiveness. These people called themselves Evangelicals. They said that the main Christian work was saving souls—making every person a Christian.

"Still other church people went even farther. They felt that every word of the Bible was put there by God—that God inspired the Bible writers, and that they put down his message word for word. They called themselves Fundamentalists. That word is somewhat like *foundation,* the concrete under a house. The Evangelicals and the Fundamentalists had big arguments with the people who believed in a social gospel.

Pam spoke up. "There wouldn't be any arguments about that in black churches," she said. "They have great revivals and people are converted. But black people know about injustice too. They know that both parts are Christian and both are in the Bible."

"*Right,* Pam," said Dr. Jackson. "It is when one group thinks that *only* its way of thinking is

Christian that we tend to let things get out of balance."

He seemed to shift mental gears then, and went on, "There are other special things about the Church in America. It is here that the Sunday schools developed. Public schools cannot teach religion. It is against the law, since our law *separates* church and state. So the churches need to be responsible for religious teaching."

Kristi and Pam and Jason talked about their own Sunday schools and how they liked the learning that went on there.

Dr. Jackson continued, "There is one more important part of the story. We have learned that many churches came into being because of divisions and separations. But in our own time, there has been movement in the other direction. Separated churches have gone back together. Some, like the Methodists who had divided, reunited. Some Lutheran groups got together into a united church. Some Presbyterians did the same. Then the Methodists united with the Evangelical United Brethren church. Other groups formed the United Church of Christ. These were all unions or *re*-unions."

"Oh, it's getting too complicated," complained Kristi. "I can't remember all the different ones."

"That's all right, Kristi. There is no need to try. But it is good to know that with all our many Christian varities in America, some of us *are* getting together. We call these *mergers*. The result, of course, is fewer denominations, but large ones."

"One thing more. Churches do not always have to merge in order to get together. They can cooperate and do things jointly while they still are separate. The best example of this is the National Council of Churches. Most of the larger groups belong. They got together so that they could do certain jobs, such as working for social justice, or encouraging Bible reading, or making new translations, or supporting Church World Service."

"What's that?" Anna asked. "It sounds familiar."

"That's the way American churches work together to send food and medicine anywhere in the world that there is special need. When there are floods, crop failures, earthquakes, war, Church World Service sends help.

"Well, that's about enough for today, don't you think? We'll meet at this same spot next time."

Chapter 22

OTHER LANDS HAVE SUNLIGHT, TOO

"Dr. Jack," said Jason, as the group arranged themselves on the grass, "I was thinking the other day."

"Thinking!" laughed Kristi. "You are always coming up with something new, Jason."

"Ahem," Jason cleared his throat in a way that clearly meant, *I'm ignoring you!* He turned again to Dr. Jackson. "What I was thinking . . . Christianity began over there in Palestine, a part of Asia. But almost all our story has been in Europe, and now in America. What about the rest of the world? It's pretty big."

"Excellent, Jason! That's exactly what we are going to do today—look at the Church around the world, especially in faraway places."

"You mean like Japan, Dr. Jack?" asked Kristi. "I saw something about Japan on TV. It must be a beautiful country, with all those pretty gardens, and temples with wavy roofs . . . and the kimonos. . . ."

"Yes, Kristi—Japan, and other places, too. Of course, the whole story of Christians everywhere is much too much for one afternoon. But we can find out why and how the Church spread. And we can hear some of the exciting stories about missionaries. Some were in Asia—in India, China, and Japan.

Some were in Africa, which people used to call the Dark Continent because it was so mysterious, so unknown. And some were in South America and on the islands dotted across the immense waters of the Pacific Ocean.

"First, a question. Why did all this happen? Why would Christians decide to spend their lives in far countries, telling people about the Christian faith?"

"I know," said Anna. "That's what Jesus told his followers to do. They should go into all the world and preach the gospel to all people. That's in Matthew."

Jeff spoke up, as though he had given some private thought to the idea. "If you have a belief and a faith that means a lot to you, you would like to share it with other people, no matter where they live. All people are God's people."

"Yes, indeed. Those are good reasons for the churches to send out thousands of missionaries. In fact, missionary work has been going on during all the centuries the Christian community has existed, ever since the time of the apostles, who were the first missionaries. There were missionaries in Egypt and Greece in early times, and in Rome, and then all over Europe. Later they came with the new settlers to the western world.

"But about two hundred years ago, the churches really got into the work in a special way. They discovered that there were still huge parts of the world where millions of people lived and died without ever having heard the good news. Somebody ought to tell them about Jesus. The church leaders said, 'Here are fields ripe for the harvest.' They felt the time was right.

"So in the nineteenth century, about the time our country was rolling along pretty well on its own, many churches around the world organized missionary societies. They sent missionaries on sailing ships along the trade routes, all around the world. Later they went on ocean liners, and still later, on airplanes. And it has been going on ever since. Millions have heard the story of Jesus and the Christian faith. And many of them have become Christians."

"Are there Christians in Japan, Dr. Jack?" asked Kristi.

"Yes, there are. Most Japanese are not Christian, though. In the past, they were Shintoist, and also Buddhist and Confucian. The number of Japanese Christians is small, but they are an active, dedicated group. In fact, some of their work makes for pretty exciting stories. Let me tell you a few of the true stories of Christian missionaries."

"Yes! Yes!" agreed his young friends.

"One of the earliest missionaries was a Roman Catholic named Francis Xavier. He is another Saint Francis, but rather different from our friend here," and Dr. Jackson leaned over to pat their favorite statue. "Francis Xavier was a Jesuit, a member of the Society of Jesus, which was started by Ignatius Loyola about the time of the Lutheran Reformation. Well, Francis sailed to India in one of those fragile little ships like those Columbus used when he sailed for America. Francis went to Goa, in India, where the Portuguese had built a trading post. He taught Christianity to the people, who in that part of India spoke a language called Tamil.

"Then he went to the East Indies, which we now call Indonesia, where the Portuguese were doing some trading in spices. There he worked with several native tribes. This was dangerous work, not only because some tribes were warlike, but because the seas were filled with pirates. On one island, he met a Japanese traveler, and afterward he felt that he was called to preach in Japan. Although Japan was far to the north, he did go there, and he planted the faith. Christianity had a hard time in Japan. It did not begin to grow until much later.

"But while Francis Xavier was there, he heard much about the huge nation of China, whose 'doors' were locked to the western world. He wanted to take his mission there, too, but he died before he could follow through. Francis Xavier was one of the greatest missionaries of the Church. He prepared the way for others in many parts of Asia.

"One important leader of nineteenth-century missions in the Protestant churches was William Carey, an Englishman. He was a boy during the time of the American Revolution. And his chief claim to fame in his boyhood was that he could quickly shinney up almost any tree that grew. He loved to straddle a high branch and look out on the world from his leafy perch.

"He was brought up as an English Baptist. Another very important part of his growing up was a book called *Voyages*. It was about the adventures of Captain James Cook. That book changed Will Carey's life. Along with the Bible, it made him a missionary. The book told of Captain Cook's sailing explorations in the Pacific Ocean, where he discovered lands nobody even knew were there. And young Will Carey was captivated. That excitement about the world, combined with his own deep faith, made Carey one of the most important missionaries.

"It was pretty discouraging at first, however. When Carey suggested that the Baptists ought to do something about the command of Jesus to teach all nations, the older ministers shushed him. 'Sit down, young man,' said one of them. 'When it pleases God to convert the heathen, he will do it without your aid or mine.' "

"I know some old people like that," broke in Kristi, who often said just what she thought, but sometimes without thinking. "They are just too old to understand anything new."

"Well, perhaps that isn't *quite* fair—but there certainly are people, young as well as old, who find it hard to change their ideas. In spite of everything, however, Carey kept at it. He had 'sticktoitiveness.'

"But by 1792, he was a leading minister himself. He preached a sermon about the idea, 'Expect great things from God; attempt great things for God.' And a year later he and his family were near Calcutta in India, with great hopes, but with little money.

"It was touch-and-go for many years. Now he really needed that sticktoitiveness. First he had to learn the difficult languages used in that part of India. And then it was seven long years before the very first convert was baptized.

"Carey spent the rest of his life in India missions. He became a professor in the new university in Calcutta and translated the Bible into several of their languages. He laid a good solid foundation for those who would come after him.

"Not all the famous missionaries were foreigners in the countries where they worked. Most were, at first, because they were the ones with both the faith and the money. But some native leaders were in mission work in those early years, too.

"One was Joseph Hardy Neesima, in Japan. His Japanese name was not Joseph, but Shimeta. He grew up in a Japanese Samurai family. They were the proud warrior class, who prized their long sharp swords. Shimeta also liked to fly kites. The Japanese are skillful makers of fine kites.

"Well, young Shimeta was a very curious fellow. He wanted to learn about the world outside Japan. It seems no one else thought that was worthwhile. So Shimeta studied English by himself and read *Robinson Crusoe*. The adults did not approve, and they tried to stop him, but that was like trying to stop the tide in the ocean. The young man kept on, even in secret. He wanted to *know*. One thing he learned was that Christians believed the world was made by a Creator God whom they called Heavenly Father. Shimeta wanted to visit America to learn more.

"Finally his chance came, but he had to go alone and in secret. He managed to stow away—to hide— on an American ship until it was well out at sea. When the crew found him, they agreed he could stay if he would work. He did—and he studied more English as well. On board that ship, he was given the name Joseph.

"In Boston, where the ship landed, he was very lucky. The ship owner took him into his own home. He helped him get an education and Joseph became a leader. When he was baptized as a Christian, Shimeta took the name of the shipowner as his middle name and became Joseph Hardy Neesima.

"Later Joseph finished college, was ordained a minister, and returned to Japan as a missionary to his own people. He also helped establish a fine new university in Kyoto. When Joseph died, he was not buried with his two Samurai swords. He had said that he now had two others that he thought were better—truth and love."

"Oh, Dr. Jack," said Pam, "that's the best story of all. I think Shimeta was a wonderful person."

Jeff smiled, noticing that Pam had used the missionary's original Japanese name. Pam is proud of her own black heritage and would think about

Neesima's right to be proud of his, he thought. And he felt warm inside.

Dr. Jackson continued with the missionary story. "There were other huge continents besides Asia. Missionaries went to Africa a little later. Perhaps the most famous missionary since Paul's time was a Scotsman, David Livingstone. He came along in the mid-1800s.

"But let's back up to his boyhood. He grew up in a poor family. When he was ten, he went to work in a cotton mill. But there scarcely ever was a child as eager to learn. After a twelve-hour day at work, he went to night school, and he read all the books he could find.

"Picture David at the age of twelve, at work in the cotton mill. His job was to walk down a long row of machinery, watching the bobbins unwind. As each bobbin ran out of thread, he had to replace it quickly. But at the end of the line, David kept his Latin grammar book. Each time he came to that point, he would read one line of Latin, and then he would say it over and over to himself as he made the next trip down the row of bobbins.

"Well, David Livingstone became a serious Christian. He was sure he wanted to be a missionary to China . . . until he met a missionary from Africa. Little was known about that continent, except that it was the source of the terrible black slave trade. David found a map of Africa to study—the best one available. It showed North Africa and the coast all around the continent, as it had been charted by sailors and traders. And it showed the tip of South Africa. All the rest—*all the rest of the whole continent*—was marked 'unknown.'

"When Livingstone became a medical doctor, he headed for the Unknown Continent. He sailed to

Cape Town, at the southern end, and from there, he marched into the unexplored interior. He discovered tribes no European had ever known about . . . people who had developed their own culture and civilization.

"One of his earliest and most shocking experiences was the witnessing of a tribal ritual—an initiation of young boys into manhood. These were boys about Jeff's age, and the initiation was the tribe's way of saying, 'When you survive this, you will be a man.'

"The boys were lined up, completely naked, except for a pair of tough mittens on their hands. The men gathered around them, and suddenly they began to beat the boys with sticks. The boys were supposed to protect their bodies with the mittens. This went on until the boys were cut and bleeding all over. Finally it was over, and their wounds were cleaned and bound up. By being brave, they were supposed to have become men.

"Livingstone thought this was cruel, and he said so to the chiefs. He told the chiefs that in Scotland, boys became men by studying and learning skills, not by cruel ordeals. Some of the chiefs agreed and changed their tribal ways. Many Africans saw what a good man Livingstone was, listened to his faith stories, and became Christians.

"Besides his work as a medical missionary, Livingstone was an explorer. He made important discoveries in the middle of Africa. He found great lakes and rivers that the outside world had never heard of . . . everyone had thought that the Sahara Desert probably covered most of the continent. Livingstone wanted to find the source of the tremendous Nile River which flows through Egypt and empties into the Mediterranean. But he died before he discovered it.

"David Livingstone lived a hard life in many ways.

Both his wife and his little five-year-old son died in Africa. He tried very hard to break up the slave trade. Many times he was in danger from both white and black slavers because he was interfering with their business. He understood and loved the black people, and they loved him.

"When the news of David Livingstone's death reached Scotland, a young girl named Mary Slessor volunteered as a Presbyterian missionary. Her childhood has been as hard as Livingstone's. When she was ten, her drunken father had beat her and driven her away from home. At eleven, she went to work in the mill, as Livingstone had done. But these hardships gave her great courage which helped her cope with awful experiences later on in Africa.

"Most folks thought that a young woman was crazy to want to go off alone on a dangerous mission to one of the wildest parts of Africa, the Calabar Coast. She was the only white woman in the village where she carried on her work.

"Before she had lived there long, she had gathered a number of children into her hut to live. They were abandoned, homeless waifs until she took them in. Among them was a pair of twins. Their mother had planned to throw them into the jungle to die. Her tribe thought that because twin birth was 'different,' the babies were the work of evil spirits.

"Everywhere Mary went, she took some of the little children with her, even on dangerous trips. She gave them the only chance they had to live and grow up. When she defied bad native customs by doing things such as saving the twins, she was in danger.

"More than once, Mary placed herself between warring tribes and persuaded the chiefs to make peace. To visit one tribe, she rode up a river in a large canoe paddled by thirty Africans. The chief welcomed her, and many in the village became Christians.

"Once she went far into the interior jungle to teach Christianity to a tribe that followed dreadful customs like boiling people in oil or making them drink poison to see whether they were guilty of some crime. People had done things like that in Europe in the Middle Ages. Mary convinced many tribal leaders to give up their violent customs and become peaceful. Some of them, too, became Christian.

"Mary Slessor died in Africa, after she had been there nearly forty years. Though she was famous and honored in Scotland, she chose to be buried on the Calabar Coast, among the people she loved."

Dr. Jackson paused in the storytelling. Jeff had been caught up in the tales of these missionaries and was unwilling to break the silence.

After a moment the Professor continued: "Mary Slessor was only one of many women who went to remote places in the world as missionaries. Another was an American woman, Isabella Thoburn. She was the ninth of ten children, and her older brother James was already a Methodist minister and missionary in India. He wrote to her, suggesting that she join him.

"Well, there wasn't really any way she could *do* that—there wasn't any group that would stand behind such a project for a woman. So Isabella encouraged a group of Methodist women to organize the Woman's Foreign Missionary Society. That was in 1869.

"The next year, the society sent Isabella and a woman doctor, Clara Swain, to India. The two spent most of the rest of their lives there, working especially for the education of girls. Girls were usually ignored in India. One Christian school she started became the Isabella Thoburn College. She and Dr. Swain were the first of a large number of women from the Methodist Episcopal Church who became missionaries."

Anna had been listening and thinking. "It seems," she said, "that becoming a missionary was about the only way a girl could serve the church. At least that way, girls could have lives that were exciting, and do good, too."

"Well, Anna, in those days, women could not become ministers in most churches. Today, more and more women have that opportunity. Changes come slowly, though, and although some groups have many women ministers, others still ordain only men.

"But as to the mission field, girls of those times could have exciting lives right here at home, too. Take Frances Willard and Lucy Rider Meyer, for example, in Chicago. Frances Willard became famous as president of the Women's Christian Temperance Union. She was also a leader in the social gospel. Lucy Meyer started the Chicago Training School, and all kinds of services for children and old people. She was active in the Methodist deaconess movement, which gave girls a chance to work with the poor and others in need in big cities. Chicago was also one of the centers where Mother Cabrini worked.

"Understand, now, it was not just these few, but thousands of Christians, both men and women, who went into mission work, either at home or around the world. That was a great century for Christian missions. And it is still going on. But now many more countries are involved in *sending* missionaries. It has become much more a two-way street, with many countries both sending and receiving witnesses to the Christian faith. We have so much to learn from one another."

Jeff looked around . . . at Dr. Jackson—at Pam—at Anna—even at Kristi and Jason. Yes, he thought. We really do learn from one another.

Chapter 23

GUESS WHO!

The boys and girls knew this would be the last meeting, because now the story of the Church had just about caught up with them. But they didn't know that the last meeting would be a party. Their parents had called Dr. Jackson and made plans to treat the youngsters to dinner out at the local Plaza, which contained a variety of eating places.

Jeff and Jason arrived with their parents, Anna with her mother, Pam with her family—including little brothers—and Kristi with her parents and a grandmother. They all piled out of cars, laughing and calling to one another. Dr. Jackson was already there and was soon introduced to the few family members he did not know.

Then Jason asked, "Where are we going to eat?"

Jeff's dad pointed toward the Hamburguesa, on one side of the Plaza, where they had reserved the courtyard. With leaves and tropical blossoms and the evening sky for a roof, the bigger-than-usual story group placed their orders and waited expectantly. Chatter passed back and forth across the table until the food arrived—and even then there was the talk and laughter of a good party.

At last they were all full (maybe too full, thought Jeff, contentedly). The group moved out into the

Plaza and gathered around a group of benches. Even the parents became quiet as everyone waited for Dr. Jackson to begin.

He cleared his throat, and Jeff thought, He really *is* a little shy! Having parents here makes him feel like that first time!

Dr. Jackson began: "Today we celebrate the end of our story of the Church." He looked around at the Plaza lights twinkling in the dusk. "The end is certainly fancier than the beginning. Remember how we got started because Pam skinned her knee on the statue of Francis of Assisi? We have followed the story all the way across that long bridge of time. We struggled along with the early Christians in Roman times. We and the medieval Christians got through by the skin of our teeth in the Middle Ages. We were right into the work of reform with Luther and Calvin and Wesley . . . and the smaller groups like the Anabaptists and the Quakers. And finally we have come to the other end of the long bridge. Jesus is there on the far side. Now we meet the people on this side. Guess who?"

All five young people spoke at once, pointing to themselves and at one another. Pam pointed to her family. Jason waved his hand grandly to include all the people in the park. "Us."

That was the answer. Here in the Plaza were the people at the end of the bridge of time.

Dr. Jackson went on: "Our story has filled that bridge full of Christians. They have all gone across in what we can call a historical pilgrimage. You and I have gone along with them. We have made many new friends on the way. Some were saints we can admire and follow. Others were not saints. But then, neither are we, and we can learn from them, also."

169

Jesus
Constantine
Pliny's letter
scroll of the Nicene
Jerome, Augustine

Pope Gregor
Augustine of Engl
Pope Gregory V
Pope Innocent I
King John,
John Wyclif,
Thomas Cranme
King James I,
Zwingli, John Calv

rick,
niface,
peror Henry IV,
g Philip II,
omas Aquinas,
asmus, Henry VIII,
een Elizabeth I,
ver Cromwell,
nno Simons

Martin
Luther

George Fox
John and Charles Wesley
Mary Baker Eddy
Harriet Ross Tubman
Walter Rauschenbusch
William Carey
Joseph Hardy (Shimeta) Neesima
David Livingstone, Mary Slessor
Isabella Thoburn

Kristi broke in. "Is now the time to answer my question, Dr. Jack?"

The professor grinned. "Yes, it is, Kristi. I see that neither of us has forgotten." Then he turned to the parents to explain: "That first day, when Pam ran into Saint Francis, Kristi asked 'What's a saint?' We have talked about several, now."

"Yes—once there was a *bad* good guy and a *good* good guy," Anna said.

"That leaves us needing a definition, I guess. Here is one I like:

> Saints are all different, but their characters are always unusual. They come from all kinds of people, but they all are alike in one way: Because of their love of God, they can rise above ordinary human beings and do very extraordinary things.

We have met some extraordinary people on our bridge, and before we really leave them, there are three things I want to say. First, I'd like us to remember how important Jesus the Christ was to everyone on the bridge—to saints and Crusaders, to Reformers and missionaries. Now when you read about Jesus in the Gospels, and when you think of him as Lord of your own life, your thinking will be made richer by remembering those who have gone before you."

Dr. Jackson paused a moment. As though to let that soak in, thought Jeff.

Then he continued. "The second is that we live in our *own* times: The *faith* doesn't change, but the *setting* does—just as it has continued to change all through our story. Augustine did not attend Vatican II. St. Francis did not know about Martin Luther, or about Martin Luther King. We *continue* to change.

"For instance, a hundred years ago, Christians in Europe and America were eager to go and preach the gospel all over the world. They still are. But today Christians in other nations around the world are just as likely to come to preach the gospel to us. They are missionaries, too.

"Christianity is for everyone who will accept it. But it does not take the same shape for everyone. Christian faith requires us to meet today's world and today's challenges. The *living out* of the faith takes new forms. So it is hard to set up Christian rules. But the one rule that Jesus taught never changes: We are to love God and our neighbor. Maybe that includes *listening* when an African or a Japanese Christian tells us about the faith."

Once again Dr. Jackson paused. Then he said, "About my third point. . . . Where are we on the bridge?"

Kristi answered, "On the other side. We are on the other side from Jesus."

"Now stop and think about where we are. It *seems* we are on the other side, doesn't it? The bridge leads from Jesus to us. But are we really *at the end*? Maybe we are still somewhere in the middle of that bridge."

"Oh, golly, Dr. Jack," exclaimed Pam, her black eyes sparkling. "Yes! There is more of the bridge up ahead. We can't see it because it hasn't happened yet!"

Jason whistled softly, and "Ohhh," Anna said, Pam's idea simmering in their heads.

"You mean," wondered Kristi, "there is more of the bridge than we can see?"

"Exactly," Dr. Jackson said. "Why should the bridge of time end with us? The story of the Christian Church is going on from here. There is more to come. How the story will go, we don't know yet. The government cannot tell us. Experts, bishops, wise people cannot tell us. Teachers and ministers cannot tell us. Fathers and mothers cannot tell us.

"Christian faith has reached us all the way from Jesus. But that faith reaches out beyond us into tomorrow. What does our faith say about tomorrow? Only this—that God will be *there, then,* too. Faithful Christians will be there. More than that, who knows?"

Jason said, "Maybe we'll have churches on the moon, or on space ships. Can God see us or hear us if we go that far away?"

"Sure, Jason," Anna spoke up. "If God made everything everywhere, he's out in space too, maybe waiting for us to get there. Maybe he thinks we humans are real slowpokes. Maybe we'll find wonderful things out there."

"Or right here at home," added Jeff. "I wish we could get a glimpse of the rest of our bridge of time, Dr. Jack. Maybe it's the best part yet."

"I hope so, Jeff. Paul wrote in his letters that there are three important parts of Christian living. First is faith. That part God gives us. Second is hope, which we have because we believe that God is out there ahead of us. Third, and most important, is love. That's what keeps us faithful.

"So let's end this lesson and this party by joining hands and forming a big circle. There's a song I would like for us to end with. I'll line it out for you, just as they did in the old camp meeting revivals. I'll sing a line, then you sing it after me, all the way through. *Young people only* on the first verse."

> Hosanna, loud hosanna
> The little children sang;
> Through pillared court and temple

The lovely anthem rang;
To Jesus, who had blessed them
Close folded to his breast,
The children sang their praises,
The simplest and the best.

"Now everyone!"

"Hosanna in the highest!"
That ancient song we sing,
For Christ is our Redeemer,
The Lord of heaven our King.
O may we ever praise him
With heart and life and voice,
And in his blissful presence
Eternally rejoice!

Jeff sighed. Good ending, he thought. Good group —good friends.

Kristi broke the silence, broke the spell. "Hooray," she shouted. "Now can we go get ice-cream cones?"

Dr. Jackson watched the family groups move off through the Plaza toward ice-cream cones, and toward whatever lay before them along the bridge of time: Jeff, the sturdy young man just entering the uneasy age of adolescence; Kristi, already a magnet for those around her; dark, sparkling Pam, with such a warm nature; handsome, fun-loving Jason; bright, quiet Anna.

It was Kristi, the eager ice creamer, who turned suddenly and ran back. Jeff, too, had turned to wait for the professor. Kristi caught his hand. "Let's have some more stories, Dr. Jack, and some more times together!"

"Who knows?" he replied. "Maybe that, too, lies waiting for us on the next arch of the bridge." To Jeff he added, "Make mine strawberry—double dip!"

A LIST OF REFERENCES

Bainton, Roland H. *The Church of Our Fathers*. Rev. ed. New York: Charles Scribner's Sons, 1950.

———. *Early Christianity*. Princeton, N.J.:D. Van Nostrand Co., 1960.

———. *The Reformation of the Sixteenth Century*. Boston: Beacon Press, 1952.

Cannon, William R. *History of Christianity in the Middle Ages*. Nashville: Abingdon, 1960.

Hudson, Winthrop S. *American Protestantism*. Chicago/London: University of Chicago Press, 1972.

———. *The Story of the Christian Church*. New York: Harper & Row, 1958.

Neill, Stephen. *History of Christian Missions*. Baltimore, Md.: Penguin Books, Penguin Paperbacks, 1964.

Richardson, Cyril C. *The Church Through the Centuries*. Reprint. New York: AMS Press, 1938.